Flying with Angels

Flying with Angels

Adventures in Microlights

Kevin Rutland

Airlife
England

DEDICATION

I dedicate this book to my Mam and Dad, my former wife Maria, my children Richard, Michael, Julie and Sandra, and to Anne. Without their love, encouragement and direction I would never have been given the chance to do the things I have done.

My Mam and Dad encouraged me to reach out and grasp life with both hands. Without the backing, patience and tolerance of Maria and my children I would never have had the opportunity to achieve my dreams of flight. Anne has given me the time, encouragement and confidence to put my thoughts and memories down on paper and to share my world with others.

Philip, Tim, Colin, Rob and all the other wonderful friends I have made during my crazy life also deserve mention, as they provide the meat on my otherwise skeletal story. I wish I could name them all, but they know who they are and will always be in my thoughts.

I also would like to add two Peters and John to my dedication – they also fly with angels.

Copyright © 2000 Kevin Rutland

First Published in the UK in 2000
by Airlife Publishing Ltd

British Library Cataloguing-in-Publication Data
A catalogue record for this book
is available from the British Library

ISBN 1 84037 136 6

Typeset by Phoenix Typesetting, Ilkley, West Yorkshire
Printed in England by St Edmundsbury Press, Bury St Edmunds, Suffolk

Airlife Publishing Ltd

101 Longden Road, Shrewsbury, SY3 9EB, England
E-mail: airlife@airlifebooks.com
Website: www.airlifebooks.com

CONTENTS

Chapter 1

CRAZY OR NOT, I'M DOING IT

I knew I was about to die. I was rushing towards the ground at 60 mph, and I had made a big mistake! I closed my eyes and waited for my life to flash by – it didn't.

There was a slow-motion sequence with sounds and feelings that I can still 'picture' today, as light metal hit the ground, bent, tore, screamed, bounced, and snapped. The sequence repeated itself twice more. Then . . . an eerie silence. Was I dead? Could I open my eyes, or was Heaven a dark place (assuming I had not penetrated the Underworld to arrive swiftly at the 'Other Place'). I felt nothing, no pain – I must be dead. I had hoped for a much longer stay on this Earth, and I should have known better than to take up this crazy pastime. I hit the ground hard, far too hard to survive. Perhaps passing into the Next World was as painless and swift as we are all led to believe.

Eventually, I dared to open my eyes and realised I was still alive, but the realisation was quickly followed by the thought that if I didn't get out of the wreckage quickly, then my life may still be drastically shortened. I could smell fuel, and the engine was making hot tinkling noises. I was fully aware that if the fuel came into contact with the hot engine, a fire would certainly follow.

However, there was one slight problem. I seemed to be trapped and could not move out of the seat. I tentatively checked my extremities to see if anything was missing or broken. The only part of my body which seemed to have a problem was my left hand, which had that broken sort of feeling. Everything else seemed fine, but I knew that my body had anaesthetised itself to give me a chance to survive the life-threatening situation I had foolishly placed myself in.

To get out I had to release the seat-belt, which had prevented me from digging my own grave after being flung at the ground at such a deadly speed. The problem was that the release buckle was now hidden underneath an aluminium tube, which was once part of the control system for my amazing machine. Finally, aware that survival was an option, I used both hands to try to push the offending tube away. At first it seemed that it was not going to move, but with the strength that comes with fear, I managed to move it sufficiently to release the buckle. I needed to move the tube much further as it was still preventing me from pulling myself out of my tailored seat. I was still not out of the frying pan, but at least the machine had not yet burst into flames. With another burst of energy I forced it just enough to wriggle past it, and dragged myself out of the remains of a once beautiful unique form of flying machine.

As they say, any landing you can walk away from is a good one, so I was delighted to have escaped from the jaws of death. I then looked back at my once beautiful little machine and decided that it was now only fit for several plastic rubbish sacks. My elation at having survived the crash turned to sadness, as I realised that I had broken the little toy that I had worked for so long to obtain.

The man who opened his door at 7.05 am that Saturday morning, only to find it was not the milk delivery man, but a fallen angel, made the whole episode seem even more unreal. In a typically British way, I was invited in, given some first aid for minor scratches and made a 'nice cup of tea'. Then the phone was made available to enable me to call up both the friends who were expecting me to arrive at their landing strip for an early breakfast, and my wife whom I had left a short time earlier.

Eventually my wife, Maria, and two 'Good Samaritan' friends

The fallen bird with broken wings.

The cows show no immediate interest and continue grazing.

arrived at the crash site, suitably equipped to remove the recently created junk heap from its resting place, and to take the battered, but far from beaten, survivor back home. I sat watching the performance and counted my blessings at surviving what had been a life-threatening experience, and pondered the financial problems I had just crashed myself into.

Chapter 2

ARE YOU OUT OF YOUR MIND?

Almost every non-flyer I talk to assumes, wrongly, that flying is a pastime enjoyed solely by the rich. It was an impression I also shared, until I attended an airshow in May 1987. I was wandering about at the Mildenhall USAF Airshow, looking at the various static displays inside one of the cavernous hangars when I saw a type of flying machine I'd never seen before. They are called microlights in Britain and Europe (or ultralights in the USA). At first glance, they looked more like part of a sailing boat, with tubes, wire and colourful Dacron fabric. And they looked so exposed and *frail*! However, on closer inspection I realised that there was some very clever engineering involved. What attracted me most was a detailed list showing the cost of owning and flying one of these unique machines.

From about fourteen years old I have harboured a dream to fly, but the problem has always been the cost of obtaining a licence, and then procuring a flying machine. I had previously looked at gliding. This appears to be cheaper than flying a powered aircraft, but there is too much sitting around waiting for a turn for my liking. Also, I tend to feel sick on simple fairground rides, so the thought of being thrown about in a glider, in turbulent rising and sinking air, didn't fill me with a desire to pursue it.

Every other form of flying seemed far too prohibitive. Obtaining a Private Pilot's Licence (PPL) in England requires forty hours of training, at about £50 ($80) per hour. Then one has to have a suitable machine to fly. With conventional aeroplanes costing £10,000 ($16,000) upwards, that would have meant buying one, or sharing one with a group of other people. However, I don't like the idea of sharing something that may have been bent by the previous occupant. Even flying in a club would cost more than I was ever likely to be able to afford. That avenue was well out of reach for a thirty-six-year-old teacher, with four children, a wife, a car and mortgage to support.

However, here in this hangar was something completely different. The information mentioned getting a licence for about £500 ($800), and the possibility of getting a second-hand microlight for about £1500 ($2400). This was still quite expensive, but something I could save up for over a couple of years, if I really tried. I just needed to find somewhere to try out this form of flying to see if I liked it, and to make sure it really was safe.

Chapter 3

A STRANGE INITIATION CEREMONY

Finding a place where microlights were available for training was not easy. I had never seen any of these machines flying, and neither had the Air Traffic Controller at Norwich City Airport. Eventually, after several false trails, Maria and I managed to find a local instructor just thirty minutes away from where we lived!

The experience turned out to be a very unusual initiation into microlight flying. The instructor was a very nervous man, who rushed around, putting his mobile phone on the ground and then worrying about where he had left it. He looked as if he would have felt more at home in the Biggles era, with his leather jacket, white scarf, and the impression that he was just waiting for the Red Baron to appear!

Nevertheless, I was determined to try out this method of flying. After he briefly explained the method of training and obtaining a licence to fly microlights, we got into his two-seat machine and strapped in for a trial flight. The strap was simply a lap seat-belt, but I felt secure with the supplied flying suit, gloves and crash helmet.

I should explain that there are two types of microlight. There is the (sometimes) conventional-looking three-axis aeroplane with one or two wings positioned about the middle of the machine. These have

13

another smaller wing back near the rudder, and the whole thing is controlled with a 'stick' and rudder pedals. This is the sort of machine everyone thinks of when the word aeroplane is mentioned. Then there is the flexwing microlight, which is the sort of machine I saw in the hangar. The flexwing evolved from hang-gliding technology, when someone added an engine to make life easier. Easier, that is, than jumping off a cliff! This type of machine has a triangular-shaped Dacron fabric wing. Beneath the wing is the power unit and cockpit area, known as the trike. To control the machine one 'moves' a control bar, which is connected directly to the wing. This control bar is a triangular frame held in place by wires attached to the wing, and is positioned comfortably just in front of the pilot's shoulders. There are no rudder pedals because there is no conventional rudder. The whole concept of microlighting is that the machines are 'very lightweight', and minimal (i.e. simple to fly).

There are single-seat microlights and two-seat ones. The latter are invariably tandem. The person sitting in the front uses the space between the legs of the back seat flyer as a backrest. It is a very 'friendly' position to adopt, and makes full use of the limited space. The person at the back sits about a foot higher than the pilot and has a wonderful view.

It is normal for the instructor to fly the machine from the back seat when giving lessons or trial flights, so that the would-be student can have a go at using the controls from the normal pilot's position. However, my instructor decided to sit in the front seat. He still seemed concerned about the whereabouts of his cell phone. We taxied forward, and I was excitedly looking forward to my second flight in any form of flying machine. (My first flight had been in a small light aircraft at a local air show several years before.) Without warning, I found myself tipped at ninety degrees to the ground admiring the greenness of the grass. Was this some sort of initiation test for the novice I wondered. Perhaps it was a test to see how I would behave under stress? No, but it was my first insight into the delicate handling qualities of microlights on the ground.

My instructor had been in the process of donning his gloves and had briefly let go of the control bar. That was all it took for the wind to take control. The air current got under one side of the wing and gently tipped the machine over onto its side. It was my first experience of dangling on a seat-belt – a taste of things to come!

The only problem with these machines is that, unlike conventional aircraft, where the stick and rudder are given 'mechanical advantages' to make controlling the effects of the elements easier, microlights work in the reverse sense. The thirty-six-foot wing is controlled by moving the weight of the trike unit around under it with the control bar, which is called weightshifting. In the air it is not a problem, but on the ground the wind can get under a wing-tip and very easily catch out the unwary pilot, unless he keeps a firm grip on the control bar.

The resulting damage to my instructor's machine was limited to some bent aluminium tubes, but the microlight was no longer safe to fly. No problem, we simply transferred ourselves to another machine. Some people would at this point have beat a hasty retreat, but as I have always been sadly lacking in brain cells this minor mishap failed to deter me, and I had one of the most thrilling moments of my life.

Microlighting is unlike any other form of flying. The closest thing I can compare it to would be motorcycling, but it would be three-dimensional motorcycling. One sits, strapped into something like a dining room chair, suspended in the air by a combination of tubes, wire and colored Dacron, and can feel the force of the air rushing by, lifting everything off the ground. The views cannot be described adequately, nor can photographs capture the thrilling feeling of being an angel, looking down on the little world below.

I often think that those who get hooked on drugs should try putting

The wonderful views that are available to any birds of the air. Loddon, Norfolk.

15

Strange patterns and colours that only become apparent when viewed from the air.

their money into flying. They will get everything they are looking for, and much more. The risk of permanent injury or death is greatly reduced and they would experience something very few others have actually had access to – microlighting is a 'clean drug'. That first flight was the start of something that was to take over and completely change the direction of my life, allowing me to experience 'mini adventures' better than any book or film I was ever likely to read or see.

Chapter 4

THINGS THAT GO UP USUALLY COME BACK DOWN INTACT

I decided that I was going to love this form of flying, but needed a less volatile instructor. So, armed with new information I headed off on a journey lasting about ninety minutes by car, to another training school I had heard about. Here they had not succumbed to cell phone technology.

Following the directions I had been given, I arrived at a large, and I mean *large*, field in the middle of the Cambridgeshire flatlands. This thrilling and friendly place was called Sutton Meadows. Several colourful machines were circling in the beautiful blue sky, dropping down to land, then launching themselves back into the air again. I later discovered that this was called 'circuit bashing' and an essential part of getting one's wings.

I met Alan Reynolds, a brilliant instructor and outstanding microlight pilot. As I was not yet able to afford to buy a machine, I fed my addiction by turning up for the occasional lesson over the next few months whilst I saved as much as I could.

I soon realised that training on a microlight was very weather dependent. Newer machines were capable of handling winds of 15–20 mph, but for training purposes winds well under 10 mph were required. I often turned up at the training field, having left my home in 'still air' conditions, only to find unacceptable conditions for training at Sutton Meadows. Learning anything takes patience and time, and microlight flying is no exception. I would read back copies of microlight magazines in the School's caravan, until the wind dropped enough to allow training to recommence. Occasionally, Alan would say it was too windy for a lesson, but would I like a flight, just for fun. Would I! Wearing strange-looking insulated suits, helmets and gloves, we would take to the turbulent skies.

Alan would show me skills and pass on advice freely. If I asked a 'What if?' question he would reply 'I'll show you what would happen'.

I must add that Alan was also a test pilot for a microlight manu-facturer, and possessed skills well beyond normal beings. I always felt safe with him and learned not only about the techniques, but also other immeasurable joys of flying. He would never charge for these flights, saying that he was going up anyway. Alan was like so many microlighters, he loved to pass on the joy of flying to everyone he met.

Once I had saved the £1500 I needed for a machine Alan guided me towards a cheap second-hand single-seat microlight, called a Triflyer 250. He explained that although it was old and slow, it would allow me to learn the skills I needed. It was a lovely little machine. I sat, totally exposed to the elements upon a cloth seat, with only a seat-belt keeping me there. There was no instrumentation. I started the little two-stroke engine by pulling a recoil start handle (similar to motor mowers and outboard motors) and flew it with a wrist altimeter strapped to one wrist and a watch on the other. I added a simple Air Speed Indicator (ASI) which I strapped to the tube in front of me. I never went far enough from my take-off point to need a compass. Its maximum speed was 30 mph, and it stalled (fell out of the sky) at 18 mph. This was very important as it also meant that it landed at about the same speed. It

I could not resist trying out the full flying gear, even with the trike still attached to the trailer.

held five litres of two-stroke fuel, which would keep it airborne for about thirty minutes safely. It was more like a bicycle than a motorbike!

Another important point about the microlight, was that the wing could be folded up to fit inside an eighteen-foot long narrow wing bag, which fitted on a car roof rack. The trike unit could be transported in a small trailer. Both items fitted nicely into my garage, thereby saving hangarage charges. Having an aeroplane that can be packed away into a small space is a definite plus for the pilot with limited funds.

During the spring of 1988, I arrived at the training field ready to begin my full training for the licence, only to find that Alan had moved on, and Dave Garrison and his son, Sean, had taken over the operation. Dave had agreed to continue training all Alan's pupils, so we started training together in April.

To keep costs low I had decided to camp on the field for a week. I wanted to get to the stage where I could go solo (be allowed to fly on my own, but under supervision). It was a strange experience to be alone on a deserted airfield, miles from the nearest pub, waking up to a frost or snow covering the ground each morning. However, it was the only way I would be able to keep the costs down and get my licence, and it was worth all the discomfort.

I should explain that there are several stages involved in obtaining a licence. One starts one's training in a two-seat machine with the instructor in the back and the first stage is achieving the standard required to go solo. The student then 'circuit bashes', practising the key basic skills, especially the vital landing stage, until he can safely control the machine and be allowed out alone. Then another period of dual training follows, where advanced skills including navigation are taught. One is eventually sent off on several solo cross-country exercises, then finally sit several Aviation Test papers and pass a General Flying Test (GFT) before one can apply for the full Private Pilot's Licence.

In those seven days Dave and Sean worked really hard to get me up to the required standard. Like most pupils I went 'one step forward and two steps back', but gradually the theory and the skills were implanted and I improved steadily. I learned how to cope with all sorts of emergencies, such as stalls and engine failures. Engine failures, especially, were thrown at me at various parts of the sessions, from just after take-off, to just approaching to land. Microlight engines are not to be totally relied on and this training proved well worthwhile on many later occasions! I owe my continued existence to this dedicated training.

Out of the seven days I had allowed myself, only the sixth was

unflyable. Sean taught me for much of the time and remained remark-
ably calm, as I fumbled my way through the various exercises designed
to prevent me killing myself or anyone flying with me. He always
seemed to have a way to get me past the mental blocks my overloaded
brain created when it was totally overwhelmed. One occasion, when I
was going to pieces every time I tried to land, he made me take off, fly
a circuit and land using only two fingertips, to demonstrate how I was
over-controlling the machine. At that moment I understood that it was
me that was sending the microlight into crazy oscillations on the final
approach, and I advanced rapidly once I realised I had been fighting
the controls rather than working with them.

Finally, I was at the stage where I could be allowed out on my own.
I will never forget the evening of the seventh day, when the wind
dropped to nothing to present me with the privilege of flying my own
aeroplane for the first time. I had sat around all day waiting for the
fresh breeze to decrease and let me become free of the earth. Just when
we were thinking of folding up the wing, the wind dropped and I was
given the chance to prove that I was able to control my own aeroplane.
I flew a complete circuit and my wheels gently touched the ground just
as a magnificent sunset began. It was pure magic.

From then on I would trailer my little flying machine backwards and
forwards to Sutton Meadows from my home a good ninety minutes
away by road. Usually, it meant sitting around drinking coffee and
talking to other pilots and trainees, sometimes for hours on end,
waiting for the wind to drop. But when the wind did relent it was
wonderful to be able to just take off, and practise and play in the area
around the training school.

I think that the people who take up microlighting are a very special
breed. No matter the occupation (not normally discussed), everyone's
love of flying would bond us all together as though we were lifelong
friends. It is one of the most appealing sides to this wonderful pastime.
Total strangers would quickly become close friends, as we told our 'tall
tales and derring-dos' or discussed hard landings and the sensation of
being tossed about the sky by the uncaring thermals.

On most occasions the wind would eventually drop enough for us to
be given permission to fly circuits and practise some of the other
manoeuvres we had been taught. In this way I gradually improved my
ability to take off, fly a controlled pattern and land. These circuits were
practised repeatedly in a variety of conditions, so that we could cope
with the usual, and sometimes unusual, circumstances we might find
once we were on our own. Watching any aircraft land is usually very
entertaining and we would critically analyse every take-off and landing.

I know I usually provided plenty of entertainment and grounds for comment.

Because of my slow, limited range machine I had decided to apply for a 'Restricted' licence. This would allow me to fly from anywhere I chose, but restricted me to a radius of eight miles from my take-off point. I did not need to do the cross-country training required for a Full Licence straight away, thus saving the cost of extra training.

However, I still had to pass the General Flying Test (GFT) and sit all the theory papers. These aviation theory papers were no problem, as I'd spent plenty of time studying the books on the wet and windy days in the caravan, or at home every evening. Taking my General Flying Test was more unusual. Because my machine was a single-seater, my instructor had to give me instructions on the ground, which I then attempted to carry out in the air. Then I would land and be given the next set of instructions.

All was going well until the engine started to misfire on take-off. I was almost through the test, but even after changing plugs and checking the fuel system the misfire kept returning. Dave put a hold on the GFT, to give me time to try and fix the problem. After checking everything once again I took the machine up for a 'Test Flight'. About seven minutes into the flight the engine started coughing and misfiring again, so I landed and fiddled again with the settings. After several more attempts, I finished the evening by having a real engine failure.

I had just taken off once again, thinking I had solved the problem. When I got to about fifty feet the engine cut out, just as I passed the edge of the landing field. The golden rule 'Never Turn Back' had been hammered into me. At this height a turn back is normally a serious mistake, if not fatal. Many inexperienced or panicking pilots have died trying to return to the piece of ground so recently left in an emergency, or after an engine failure. With no power and minimal airspeed the likelihood of a stall during the turn is very high, so I tried to make the best landing of my life into the wheat field just ahead of me. Indeed, I do believe it *was* the best landing of my life. The machine settled down gently onto the crop, stopping in only a few feet, with no damage to the microlight or myself.

I then spent almost four months trying to remedy the engine problem. At home, I would run the engine on the ground for twenty minutes at a time without a hitch. However, as soon as I returned to Sutton Meadows to fly once more it would play up again, and it always seemed to happen about seven minutes into the flight. I would have just turned into the downwind leg of the circuit when the engine would stop. No problem, I just glided the rest of the way round the circuit to land once again and tried to find the elusive fault. Eventually, I replaced the condensers and cured the problem, but not before I had learned my lesson the hard way.

Over-confidence is a very dangerous thing, and now that I had become so adept at 'engine off' landings I was extremely over-confident. On about the tenth circuit, involving the usual seven-minute engine failure followed by a glide back onto the field, I became so sure of myself that I decided to touch down about one foot beyond the edge where the grass had been lifted for lawn turf. I was so good at these glide approaches that I knew I could land within inches of my chosen spot. But not this time.

I hit the edge of the turf cut line itself and was catapulted back into the air a good six feet. I hoped no one had noticed, as I finally settled back on the ground. But pride wasn't the only thing likely to be damaged here, and it was only when I got out to inspect the microlight that I realised I had done some major damage to the machine itself. The front strut, an aluminium tube between the front of the trike and the point where the wing was attached, was bent forward like a banana.

Microlights rely heavily on triangles to give them their strength and rigidity. Further close inspection of my machine revealed that the base tube running under the seat was also bent, and the pylon (the tube up to the wing) was also showing signs of distortion around the engine mounts. I would also need to have the wing inspected as well, as the shock loads would have run up the pylon and had probably bent some of the main tubes that made up the wing. The end result was a total stripdown of both the wing and the trike, a four-month wait for replacement aircraft quality tubes and a big hole in my pocket.

My confidence was severely dented too, so I booked myself for more training, and arranged to take the GFT in the flying school's machine. Dave put me through burning hoops over the next couple of days, as I had a mental block on the simulated engine failure exercises and needed to be coaxed out of my frozen state. I was finally granted a pass, after dozens of 'engine failure' situations during the test.

Chapter 5

FLYING WITH REAL PILOTS

Once I had been granted my PPL (Private Pilot's Licence) I was free to fly without supervision. In January 1989 I went to the local flying club, near my home in south-east Norfolk, and was accepted as a special member. There had been a previous microlight member, several years before, who had scared many members when he crashed badly on the airfield. It was therefore with some reservations that I was allowed to fly from their 'General Aviation' airfield.

Because of my slow flying machine and odd flying clothing I was shunned by several of the 'real' pilots, who regarded microlighting as a 'noisy and offensive pastime carried out by untrained and unqualified cowboys'. They seemed to know very little bout the licensing require- ments and acted in a very superior way. Fortunately, not everyone held that opinion, and I was treated with respect by the more knowledge- able members of the club.

For the next six months I enjoyed some lovely 'light winds' flying. I would arrive on early mornings, or calm afternoons, rig up the wing and attach it to the trike. After climbing into my one-piece flying suit, donning the crash helmet, insulated boots and gloves, and attaching a Plexiglas map board across my knees, I was able to fly around the local area up to about two miles from the airfield, before cold, or more likely lack of fuel, would force a return to base.

Then the day came when my machine and I had to part company, although it was a parting in more ways than one! I had just taken off, and was about five hundred feet above a lovely wheat field, with the end of the runway several hundred feet behind me. As I eased off on the foot-operated throttle and commenced a slow left turn, the propeller took on a life of its own. It decided to take its leave, complete with drive shaft, drive pulleys and belts. I didn't have time to see where it had decided to go as I was busy with the more urgent problem of landing my recently converted glider. The engine over-revved, so I promptly shut it down, realising that there was a distinct lack of any propeller noise behind me. I hoped it hadn't exited through the wing.

23

I was at a safe enough height to turn back, and as I was already turning anyway I continued to turn fully towards the runway I had just left. Fortunately there was no wind, as landing downwind greatly increases the landing speed, and can also be hazardous. I glided down and landed safely, with no damage, except a few more grey hairs.

I had been over a huge ripening wheat field at the time the propeller decided to leave me, and I was concerned that a combine harvester may become damaged by taking it up into its innards. Therefore, apart from reporting it to the local policeman (who was also a member of the flying club), I spent several days walking along the tractor lines in the field searching the three-foot high crop for signs of the propeller.

Some weeks later the policeman told me that a local gamekeeper had found it about a quarter of a mile away in a wood, at the edge of the large wheat field. The gamekeeper had said that he had propped it against a tree. I had also searched the wood but never found it.

Chapter 6

MOVING UP (AND DOWN) IN THE WORLD

This most recent structural failure made me realise that it was time to move on and get a more modern machine; one that would allow me to travel further afield. I was getting fed up with the unreliability of my old Triflyer, and wanted to complete my Full Licence so that I could take up cross-country flying. By taking out a loan I could just about afford the latest design of a single-seat high performance machine called a Chaser. It was a totally different flying machine.

It cruised at 60 mph, had a Never Exceed speed of 108 mph, could climb at well over 1000 feet per minute, and had a duration of three-and-a-half hours on twenty-five litres of fuel. It was a serious flying machine. It was also very easy to fly, rig and derig. Many of the two-seat machines available, apart from being more expensive, have very large wings, which makes them hard to rig alone. If they are flown solo, ballast must often be carried. Unfortunately, there did not seem to be anyone else around when I was going flying! I therefore decided on the Chaser – it was the perfect machine for me.

I discovered that my first instructor, Alan Reynolds, was the local dealer for these machines. He had set himself up again at the Crowfield Gliding Club in Cambridgeshire, proving once again that microlights can mix successfully with all other forms of aviation. I collected my machine from him, having first had a good briefing about its different handling characteristics.

It was a dream of a machine to fly, once I got used to the much faster landing approach speed. It would approach at 55 mph and land at about 35 mph. It had a very short wheelbase, and it was a machine known to need careful handling when taxying. I personally never found it to be a problem, and loved it.

In order to get my Full Licence I first had to complete my Practical Navigation Tests. I experienced forces of Nature, that will be forever imprinted on my mind, whilst flying into a thunderstorm during my qualifying cross-country navigational flight. A thrilling and scary experience, it was also a bizarre one.

It was July 1989, one of the hottest periods of glorious summer in England in many years. The days had been exceedingly hot for several weeks, but at last there were signs of the thunderstorms that usually put an end to such weather. I was to fly from the gliding club site at Crowfield in Cambridgeshire to my own flying club (near Norwich in Norfolk), land and refuel, and then return to Crowfield.

I set off with some trepidation on this long navigational flight, likely to last over two hours in each direction. It was *very* hot and I was not too certain that the weather pattern was going to last, so I arranged with Alan to stop off overnight at my home airfield if the weather broke, instead of returning to Crowfield. The visibility was excellent and the upper air cool and comfortable as I cruised along at an airspeed of 60 mph. It was a delightful first leg; I found my turn points easily and arrived at my home base around lunchtime.

After a short stop to refuel, I asked about the possibility of the weather breaking, and was reassured that there was no likelihood of any change, so I set off on the return journey. As I got within twenty miles of my destination I became increasingly alarmed at the sight of massive cumulus clouds ahead, pumping up thousands of feet into the beautiful blue sky. Even more disturbing were the occasional flashes of lightning bursting out from the base of this huge monster of a cumulo-nimbus.

It seemed to be swelling up right in front of me. The air felt full of static, and within a few moments I was being tossed up hundreds of feet and then back down again. I had read about hang-glider pilots being sucked up into thunderstorms and being killed by the incredible forces inside these terrifying beasts of violent, boiling air. I was about fifteen miles away from this example of Nature's awesome power, and I did not like it one little bit. I could not escape its clutches and became scared of the awesome and totally unavoidable display of raw energy. I hurriedly decided to land – anywhere would do. Directly below me was a very large pea field that had recently been harvested, and in the distance I noticed a Happy Eater cafe. There was no time to deliberate any further, I simply wanted to be on the ground.

The landing was excellent, although I did have to pass under some power cables strung across the field. I taxied up to the farm buildings to explain my uninvited arrival. Strangely, there was no one about. The farmhouse door was unlocked, but I did not feel right about wandering into someone's house without permission, so I sat down, waiting for the owners to return. I decided to derig the machine to prevent it from being torn apart by the rogue winds which were now

Even this threatening-looking picture cannot not fully portray the potentially destructive power of thunder clouds.

everywhere. I dropped the wing to the ground and waited for the storm to pass.

I waited and waited but the storm worsened. There was no rain, but the winds and constant flashes of lightning kept me firmly on the ground. It was incredibly hot and I was getting thirsty and hungry – I had not prepared for a full day out and had left my lunch and drinks at Crowfield. The cafe in the distance looked inviting, so I decided to go over and get some food. I could also call home and let both my wife and my instructor know where I was. It was only when I tried to walk across the field that I realised that I had landed on the wrong side of a huge water-filled dyke. I would have to walk several miles round by road to get to the cafe, so the food would have to wait.

Back at the farmhouse there was still no sign of anyone. I stayed up until 11.00 pm, watching the best ever display of lightning I had ever seen, expecting the farmer to return home at any time. By then I was so tired and hungry I simply wanted to settle down somewhere and go to sleep. I therefore spent the night in the barn on an old settee, devoid of coverings. The stuffing had been removed and all that was left was a skeletal frame complete with rusting steel springs. I found a couple of planks to put on top of the bare springs, added my flying suit and spent a very restless night, as the thunder crashed and the lightning flashed.

I was up at 5.00 am but there was still no sign of the farmer. I decided to set up the microlight and finish the rest of the flight. Arriving at Crowfield, I had to wait until 8.00 am for someone to arrive. It was a very hungry man who was first in line for breakfast as soon as the club-house opened that morning. I found out later that the local town, just five miles from where I spent the night, had had over four inches of rain that evening. I never did discover who the owner of the farm was, or where he was that night. He probably never knew about the stranger who slept in his barn.

However, the experience taught me many things. I now always travel with a supply of food and water. I also *never* venture out if there is any possibility of thunderstorm activity. The effects can often be felt twenty or more miles from a thunderstorm, as it sucks up air and then dumps it. Carrying a mobile phone is also a very sensible idea (they were not cheaply available at that time).

Chapter 7

FLYING WITH ANGELS

I spent the next two years simply flying for fun. Microlighting is a drug, the fix is to get up into the sky. Every moment of every day I would be watching the clouds, keeping a close eye on all weather forecasts. I soon developed the basic skills necessary to spot a possible flying day. Usually, a weather forecast that predicted an excellent weekend a few days ahead would invariably mean that the whole weekend would be howling gales, fog, torrential rain, snow, or a combination of all of them. By studying the isobar charts I became more able to guess the likely pattern of winds for the following days.

Even the Friday night forecast could not be totally relied upon. It was as if the weather knew that all over the country crazy people were planning to rush into the air, and needed to be prevented for their own good. I would often stay up for several hours on a Friday night phoning owners of grass strips to get permission to visit them. Then I would phone around all my similarly afflicted friends to see if any were intending to fly, so that we could group together and make a day of it. Finally, I would sit down and plan my routes, working out headings to fly based on various wind speeds. Very often, all this planning would be wasted as an unpredicted weather front moved in to bring conditions that not even a madman would venture out in.

However, on the perfect days, when all the planning and preparations were rewarded with a correct forecast, I would be up at 6.00 am, then out on the airfield rigging the wing and attaching it to the trike. Once I had performed a careful inspection to make sure everything was exactly as it should be, I would mix up the two-stroke fuel and fill the tank. If I was likely to be travelling far I usually tried to ensure that there would be fuel available for my journey home, or to allow me to travel onward to my next port of call.

By 7.30 am I would be ready to put on my layers of clothing and flying suit. These suits are designed with two long zips running from the neck to each ankle. These zips enabled the wearer to wander around with the suit either unzipped to the waist, or loose around the legs, when moving about on the ground. Without this facility I would soon become a slowcooker, and be in meltdown mode by the time I was ready for flying. Even so, any delay once I settled into the machine would cause me to overheat rapidly.

I used to wear several layers of clothing because I liked to fly high. Usually, if I got above three thousand feet in the winter or six thousand feet in the summer I could get above the turbulence that threw these little machines about. Above what is known as the inversion layer, the air would be silky smooth, and one could let the machine fly itself with very little control input required. The downside was that the air was much cooler and the temperature soon made flying unpleasant if one was not well insulated. So, with my layers of clothing, inner and outer gloves and insulated boots I was prepared for the cold aloft. If I found it was too warm I could simply open the zips to allow a cooling breeze to force its way around the suit.

With the Chaser I had to start the engine whilst still outside the machine. A vital check was to ensure that the throttle was set in the idle position. I had seen someone being dragged along after starting the machine with the throttle advanced – he was lucky not to fall into the path of the propeller. The starting technique involved making sure no one was too close, checking the throttle, switching on the ignition, shouting 'Clear prop', and pulling on the recoil starter (just like on many outboard motors or lawn mowers). Once the engine was running evenly I would quickly hop in, secure the lap seat-belt, attach the map board, and carry out essential control movements to ensure that nothing was caught up. Then I was ready to go. Once in the air I would throttle back and ease into a gentle climb and level off at the circuit height, until I was clear of the airstrip. Once clear I could continue my climb to my desired altitude.

Microlights take off very easily, and rarely need more than about one hundred yards of grass to take off from. Any field can be used, providing you have the owner's permission, which is one of the advantages of flying such a lightweight machine. Taxying in a gentle breeze is not a problem, and once lined up and pointing into the wind all one needs to do is increase the throttle. Within a few moments one is off the ground and climbing at about one thousand feet per minute.

I love flying high, not just to avoid the turbulent air, although that is the main reason, but also because it provides such wonderful views of the countryside. Everything looks so different and I always feel closer to God, as if I am flying with His angels. Flying for fun is a privilege that few people are able to experience. It is nothing like flying in a commercial aircraft, or even a smaller private aeroplane. Seeing the world in this way, feeling the rush of air that is helping to keep me up there is, for me, very special. The feelings are beyond words, and one must experience it to understand.

Most pilots prefer to fly at between 500–3000 ft, the majority preferring to fly at 1500 ft. Many pilots will say they feel safer at 500 feet, but it is actually much safer to fly higher. If the engine stops you have much more time to sort yourself out and pick a suitable landing field. Humans have developed a blind faith in modern engines, but I know that any engine can and will eventually stop. One should always be prepared for that moment. Believe me, I know what I am talking about! Although I must keep a good lookout for other aircraft at this altitude, I am usually alone. Indeed, on many occasions I see no other aircraft. At 5000 ft I am one mile high, and in another world.

The sky has sights normally hidden from ground dwellers. I have had many types of birds flying alongside me, especially when soaring, that is, circling in rising currents of air. The most amazing thing I ever saw was when I was training. Having landed after a flight, I found I was covered in what I call Angel's Hair, i.e. thin strands of spider threads. It seems that some spiders also like to fly. They put out a length of thread into rising air and are swept aloft, where they are carried along with the currents. I assume that they can reduce the length of the thread and control their flight level. I have come across this phenomenon several times when flying high. Literally hundreds of spiders would hitch a ride at several thousand feet, covering me with an Angel Blanket.

Flying along in the company of other machines is tremendous fun. One develops a trust of one another's ability. Usually, plans are made on the ground to decide on the leader, the height to fly and the destination. Once in the air a loose chevron is formed, with each machine in the group positioning himself just behind and slightly above the person in front, which allows everyone to keep together. The reason for flying above the person in front is to avoid the invisible wake turbulence which rolls off any aeroplane. If changes need to be made, simple hand signals allow you to move around safely.

Every site we would visit was either a training school, club site, or private strip, where we would relax, chat and take in refreshments. Most strips belonged to local farmers who loved to fly, and who usually had several flying machines on their fields. Every flyable weekend could bring visits from old friends and new ones. The whole microlight movement has evolved from this very informal method of flying into other strips, and most flyers are careful not to cause any upset in neighbour-sensitive areas.

It is a pity that there are people who want to stop anyone from enjoying their free time. I have always flown in a way to try to avoid causing disturbance. I always fly in different areas on different occasions, and I also try to fly high enough to be unheard, whenever possible. Indeed, on many occasions I have flown over friends' houses only to be told later that they did not hear me. Even when flying circuits, I usually try to vary the direction and pattern size to avoid repeatedly laying down a noise blanket over anyone's house.

Those who complain seem quite happy to use a motor mower, or other noisy implement around their houses without any thought to their neighbours' peace and quiet, but are the first to complain about anything that gives pleasure to someone else. All microlights in Britain have to carry a Noise Certificate stating that they comply with Civil Aviation Authority (CAA) regulations. Microlights are actually now quieter than most light aircraft (which do not have any noise restriction regulations).

These intolerant people seem to think that their rights are being violated. All aircraft must fly at least five hundred feet above a person, vehicle, vessel or structure, apart from when taking off and landing. There are those who worry that they can be seen when sunning themselves in their garden, but the view from five hundred feet is very poor. Try walking down the road for that distance and look back at the detail you can pick out – it really is very little. I have always been a believer in live and let live. If anyone has a problem with someone else, often the easy solution is simply to go and chat about the situation. Many pilots do try to keep well away from sensitive areas if they know about them.

I flew with friends or alone at every possible opportunity. My wife and children would often see me preparing maps and planning new places to visit on a Friday night, then see little of me for the rest of the weekend. I was also lucky, being a teacher, to be able to fly during the school holidays. Colin Lowe, a friend, policeman and very keen pilot of both light aircraft and microlights, would often fly along with me, or I would navigate for him in his two-seat machine. He worked shift patterns that allowed him to feed his addiction at similar times to mine. Summer evenings were also very pleasant for local flying, and I would rush home to try to get an hour or two in the air before it became too dark to see. On a couple of occasions I was almost caught out by fading light, but more about that later.

To keep a Pilot's Licence legal it is required that both light aircraft and microlight pilots must fly a minimum of five hours in any thirteen months. I know of many light aircraft pilots who struggle to find the money to maintain this minimum, as the cost can be prohibitive. Over the years I have flown around fifty hours or more every year, due to the very low operating costs of microlighting. Often, the only limitation is the unfavourable weather.

Once you have a microlight, maintaining it yourself is usually not too expensive compared with a light aircraft. All maintenance work can be carried out by the pilot and is signed off by a BMAA (British Microlight Aircraft Association) Inspector, which allows the running costs to be kept very low. The inspection together with a yearly check flight amounts to less than fifty pounds, and many inspectors only charge beer money to do this work.

My main expenditure each year would be for the high quality synthetic two-stroke oil that I used, together with the car grade petrol obtained from any garage. Other than that I would need replacement spark plugs and a cylinder head gasket set to allow me to carry out an engine decoke. Little else was necessary, unless I managed to bend the machine.

Chapter 8

WE ALL MAKE MISTAKES

Flying the Chaser brought many hours of pleasure. The thunderstorm incident was placed in an accessible part of my brain for future reference, and my skills improved as I clocked up hours. My navigation skills also steadily improved as I took myself further and further away from my local airfield. I was getting good at this!

One of my favourite regular outings was a nice one-and-a-half-hour flight to my old training school at Sutton Meadows. One could always guarantee a friendly afternoon spent chatting with the local pilots over a few cups of coffee, before a lovely return flight. It involved a simple flight with one turn point. I had flown this particular flight, across very featureless areas, several times and I had worked out the navigational calculations so often that I could do them in my head. The wax crayon red line I would follow was clearly drawn on my aeronautical map, together with the times to arrive at key points along the route, and the new bearing for the only turn I would have to make about halfway into the flight. It was 'piece of cake' flying.

I set out at 6.30 am on this particular morning to join a bunch of flyers at Sutton Meadows, who had planned a cross-country outing north into Lincolnshire to visit another club, which was having a fly-in barbecue. Little did I know it was going to be a day to remember.

I carefully folded my map to fit neatly into my transparent map board, which was attached to the machine to stop it blowing away in the 60 mph slipstream. It is vital in a microlight to attach everything securely to either the machine or oneself. Anything that becomes loose can and almost certainly will find its way through the propeller, with dramatic results. I had enough of the map visible to allow me to fly my normal route, allowing about ten miles either side, to help me identify landmarks along the route. Everything went to plan, right up to the first turn point.

When I turned onto the new heading, something did not feel right. I was worried about blundering into the often active RAF airfield at Marham. It is permissible (but not advisable) to stray into the airspace near to an active military airfield. However, even at weekends, when the RAF seem to all go home, it is still wiser to keep away from the 'Big Boys' Playing Areas'. With this thought in mind, and the feeling that the wind direction must have changed, I decided to head slightly more south, just to be on the safe side. Going too far south would also be a mistake, as the Army have a Battle Training Ground around Thetford Forest. Again, whilst possibly quiet at weekends, one can never rule out 'special operations' activities, and aircraft should also give this area a wide berth.

I still had the feeling that I was being pushed too far north, so I altered the heading again. By now I seemed to be flying over an area that I had not flown over before. When uncertain of one's position, the easiest thing to do is continue flying in the assumed correct direction, until a landmark is recognised, or can be identified on the map, so that is what I did. I was slightly concerned when the first easily identifiable feature I saw was a railway line – I had never seen one before in this area. Soon a fairly large town also appeared out of the haze. I frantically scanned my map to work out where I had strayed. With a sudden sinking feeling I realised that I must have overcompensated, and was heading straight for Thetford. I had blundered straight across the Battle Area.

It was now easier and safer to carry on, re-routing myself to Sutton

Meadows by flying south of the battle zone and also clear of the Mildenhall USAF airfield. I had flown this route a couple of times before, so again felt comfortable as I had re-established my position, and could do some mental calculations to get me safely to Sutton Meadows.

In fact, I was not too comfortable, as by now the chilly air was affecting my bladder, with the result that I felt a fairly urgent need to land and relieve myself. I looked at a possible landing field, near Newmarket, but aborted the landing after the first pass revealed very rough-looking clumps of bushes in the selected landing area. I decided to press on.

My mental calculations told me that I should see Sutton Meadows at any moment, but I was rather confused to see what looked like a large area of water ahead. I knew that this area of Cambridgeshire was prone to flooding in the winter time, but it was very rare to see so much water in the summer. Because of my very careful map folding, I was at this stage flying by memory, as the required piece of map was neatly tucked away under the map board, and it is almost impossible to unfold a map when flying. No problem, I knew the area, didn't I?

Finally the awful realisation dawned on me that I had again over-corrected south when I chose my new heading. What I could see in the distance was Graffam Water, well to the south-west of Sutton

A quiet field – ideal for a picnic when you want to get away from everyone (or cannot find them).

Meadows. By now my bladder was in control of all flying operations, so I decided to make a hasty landing in the disused parking area of Huntingdon race course. Fortunately, there was no one around to see my frantic efforts to remove my gloves, unzip my flying suit, etc. with numb fingers and a compelling urge.

Once able to focus on the problem, I had no difficulty refolding the map, drawing on a new track, and correctly calculating the heading required to get me to Sutton Meadows. As I approached (from the south) I could see the group of microlights taking off and heading north. They had obviously decided that I was not coming and were on their way. No problem I thought, I had a fast machine, so I could land, refuel, mark up the new track and be off again. I was certain I would catch up with them.

I was certain later that day that I did find the right place, but decided that they all must have become lost, as I could not see anyone on the ground where the barbecue should be. (In reality of course, I had blundered again.) Never mind, I had a lovely picnic in a friendly farmer's field, and flew home a much wiser pilot.

This episode taught me a very valuable lesson about becoming complacent about my skills. I resolved to 'tune' my navigation techniques so that I would never make so many basic blunders again. I also decided that a radio was a very useful extra for these situations. With a radio, I could have called up one of several radio stations to get a fix and a heading to guide me safely on my way. Consequently, I resolved to take a radio operator's course.

I should point out that it is not compulsory to carry a radio in an aeroplane. Most people who do not fly are amazed that it is not a requirement, until they realise that having a radio, and being tuned into one station, does not necessarily make flying safe. There is no common radio frequency which everyone can listen in to, or talk on, as each airfield has its own frequency and different radio-equipped aircraft will be listening to different frequencies. There does tend to be a certain complacency among radio users that they will be informed of any aircraft near them. This certainly is not always the case.

I remember flying the Triflyer one day and having a light aircraft fly so close to me that I could see the pilot bent over the radio. He had his head in the cockpit, and never saw me! I was within thirty feet of his wing. Over-reliance on radios and other electronic aids can be dangerous. I know of many light aircraft pilots who rarely look at a map, relying instead on radio beacons called VORs. They fly to one beacon and then to the next until they are near enough to their destination to ask the airfield controller for final instructions. It doesn't require much imagination to picture several aircraft all 'blindly' flying along radio signals to beacons, like bees aiming at the honey-pot, with some pilots blissfully unaware of the dangers as they fiddle with their electronic toys.

Looking around is the most important part of flying safely. Every additional piece of equipment that improves a person's chance to be alerted to danger is well worth having, providing that it does not distract one from the object of the exercise – to fly the aeroplane safely.

Chapter 9

FLYING FROM A GRASS STRIP IN THE TRUE SPIRIT OF FLYING

It was in January 1991 that I discovered what real flying was all about, flying from a grass strip! I was lucky to have a friend at my local flying club, a local policeman, who knew all the local farmers well. For the past few years I had been trailering my microlight about ten miles over to the airfield from home. Then I would spend thirty minutes setting up the wing from its wing bag, attaching it to the trike before flying. It would take another thirty minutes to carry out this operation (in reverse) at the end of the day's flying. I did not really mind this, except on cold winter days when my fingers would be frozen after completing the task. It also limited my evening flying as I had to allow time for this rigging and derigging. What I was really on the lookout for was a local farmer who would let me fly from a field nearer my home. This is where the local policeman came in. He came to me one day and said he knew of a farmer, with his own grass strip, who might be willing to let me fly from it. The great news was that I only lived about one-and-a-half miles from the farm.

When I visited the farmer, Philip Warde, at a lovely old place called Grove Farm, he was very cautious about having a microlight on the farm, but said that I could fly from the strip on a trial basis. If any local neighbours complained I would have to go. There was another great unexpected bonus, Philip had an old 'hangar'-type building in which I could keep the ready rigged wing. It was not tall enough to leave the machine fully rigged, but putting the wing onto the trike only took a couple of minutes and so it was not a problem. I asked about rental for the arrangement and he said he would wait and see how I got on first. Philip had his own light aircraft, a Piper Cub, and had a refreshingly open attitude to all forms of flying.

Flying from grass really is the true spirit of flying. It is also kinder on microlights as concrete is very unforgiving following a heavy landing, whereas grass tends to cushion the contact points, often several in any one landing. The grass strip was well over seven hundred yards long, running east/west, and was lovingly cut by Philip at regular intervals. This was far more runway than I needed, but I was taught to always make sure I had every inch of usable runway in front of me, so I always taxied right up to the very end before any take-off.

Being able to keep the wing ready to use was brilliant, and I soon devised a simple trolley to keep it off the ground. As rats are a common

The Chaser outside the simple hangar at Grove Farm.

37

problem on any farm, I didn't want to be providing a dacron meal for any of these creatures. The trolley was also great to move the wing about, saving me from carrying it very far. I could also keep the trike in the same hangar, and Philip and I put up a tarpaulin on the front to keep out the worst of the weather. I was able to lift this with a series of ropes in a couple of minutes. The wind was able to blow through the many cracks in the corrugated walls and roof, keeping the interior dry and fresh. Now I was able to go flying in about ten minutes, and had gained almost an hour by not having to drive so far, or spend time rigging/derigging.

The arrangement we had was simple. I was to arrive at the farm and go round to the hangars without disturbing Philip or his family, in other words, just get on with the flying and not interfere with their activities. This worked out perfectly, as I was able to come and go without feeling that I had to report in every time. Usually, Philip would wander over for a chat at some stage during the day. The freedom of having my 'own grass strip' opened up wonderful opportunities. I could now fly on summer evenings, or arrive at the crack of dawn and be away on long cross-country flights as soon as there was enough light.

Philip wandering over to talk to Nigel, the owner of G-NCUB.

There was a second Piper Cub on the farm, owned by Nigel, another enthusiastic grass strip flyer, who would often try to find a few minutes per day to get in some airtime. I would often arrive to see Nigel pass overhead in his classic yellow machine. He was also addicted to the wonders of flying, making full use of his antique World War Two restored aeroplane.

Although the grass strip ran east/west, the winds would vary during the year and favour almost every other point of the compass at some stage. This allowed me to develop the very important skill of crosswind landing. Ideally, an aircraft should take off and land directly into wind, which makes controlling the machine much easier, and allows for the slowest ground roll speeds. Once the wind is from another direction, life becomes much more complicated. It will try to swing the aircraft so that it points into the wind. If this is not the same direction as the runway, then constant control inputs are required to stop the machine taking a trip off into the surrounding crops. Tailwheel aircraft are especially prone to do this, but nosewheel aircraft like my Chaser had less of a problem.

It is usual to keep the machine on the ground longer when taking off in crosswind conditions, to build up speed so that one can 'pop' the aircraft up into the sky quickly. Once airborne the machine will try to turn into wind, but any turns near the ground are usually unwanted and can be dangerous. The extra groundspeed gives the pilot more airspeed and, in turn, more control caused by the airflow over the control surfaces. When landing an aircraft a pilot tries to fly into wind, which reduces the speed over the ground, resulting in a shorter landing roll. Crosswind landings also require a special technique and pilots develop their favourite methods of handling these often challenging moments.

One of the big mistakes most pilots make at least once (or more often if they have a low learning curve), is to land downwind. As soon as you try it you know something is not quite right. Even in the lightest of winds, the ground seems to rush by much quicker, and the landing roll is much longer than normal. Many pilots have run out of runway in this way. This is why you see a windsock on every active runway, as they help pilots to work out the best direction to take off and land. As my flying skills improved, I was able to attempt harder crosswind take-offs and landings.

The second year I was there Philip decided to put down a north/south second runway, which would allow us to pick the best possible take-off/landing direction for any given wind. It also removed the stress caused to a machine when taking off or landing in a crosswind.

I was very grateful for this addition, as it allowed me to fly when the crosswind was too strong for the existing east/west runway.

Chapter 10

It's Getting Dark Up Here!

Over a period of time I started to meet the other local microlight flyers, who would invite me back to their strips. This opened up new places to fly to, and I always enjoyed dropping into the nearer places for a coffee and a chat on a suitable summer evening.

I had a good friend, Rob Alston, living about an hour's flying time away near Cromer on the North Norfolk coast, and I loved to drop in to see him from time to time. He also loved to fly his Flash 2 Alpha flexwing microlight during the evenings after he had been working on the farm, and would often be taking someone up for a flight around the local area when I arrived. He always had spare fuel, or if not, would be willing to run me down to the filling station a couple of miles away.

On the particular night in question, I arrived to see him flying around in the distance. After landing we sat and drank a couple of cups of coffee and chatted about the previous week's aerial gossip. I eventually remembered that I needed some extra fuel to fly back safely. I always like to fly with full tanks, even if I have enough for the flight, as it means one less thing to worry about if things start to go wrong. Rob had just used up his spare fuel, but was willing to take me down the road to get some more. By the time we had returned and refuelled, the time had ticked by considerably.

The Chaser is a fast machine. To make a flexwing fly at a maximum speed you pull the control bar as far back as possible, but you have to simultaneously increase the engine speed. This combination makes the machine stay in level flight and go faster. The first half of the flight was fine, and I enjoyed the developing red sunset and the peace and serenity of being at one with my environment. There was still a gentle breeze, which being from the south was reducing my groundspeed slightly, but this was no real problem. Then I began to notice that the headlights of cars below were being switched on. Because of the curvature of the earth it always gets darker close to the ground than it does higher in the air. After a few minutes I could see street lights coming on automatically. Finally, understanding penetrated my peaceful subconscious, and I began to get a little concerned.

I had to get back to my grass strip before it was too dark to be able to judge the height above the ground when landing. 'I 'bent' the control bar round my stomach and revved the engine, thankful for the extra fuel, even though it was the refuelling that had cost me time, as the engine was now gulping it down as I flew at the maximum speed possible. I was within about ten miles of the strip now, and I saw the carpark lights come on in the Safeway supermarket three miles beyond my destination. It still seemed a long way away.

I started to consider my options. The situation was not yet critical. I could pick a field below, land and find a phone. However, it would mean leaving the aircraft overnight, or getting the trailer and derigging it. I decided that it was not ideal. The next option was to divert to another farmer's strip about three miles ahead, definitely a wise and sensible choice. The third option was to head for my old flying club, where landing lights had recently been installed which could be operated remotely with my radio. I decided this was the possible backup I needed and so pressed on to my strip which was still too far away to pick out clearly. 'Press-on-itis' had got many people into trouble in the past, and I was trying to avoid becoming another statistic, but I still had all these options open, so I still felt reasonably happy about continuing on to the farm.

Then an idea struck me. I radioed Grove Farm and asked them to drive a car onto the runway, point north and switch on headlights. This would hopefully confirm that I was at least flying in the right direction. A few moments later two beams of light appeared, exactly where I thought they should be. Now I had definite confirmation that I was indeed heading for the right location, in the rapidly darkening sky – one problem solved. I knew where I was going in the gathering gloom.

It was a race against the setting sun. Officially an aircraft may fly until thirty minutes after sunset. At least I was still legally entitled to be flying, even if Nature did not comply with the regulations and was withdrawing daylight before the end of the legal period. Fortunately the southerly headwind was now my friend, as it allowed me to land straight ahead, but I only had one chance at it (otherwise, I was committed to a night landing at the club airfield). Lining up on the twin beams of light, from a mile out, I touched down with just enough visibility to make out the ground sufficiently to flare the aircraft at the right moment to pull off a good landing. I checked my watch and saw that I had landed with just six minutes to go until official darkness. There had not even been enough time to carry out a go-around. Another important series of lessons had been learned, and imprinted on my brain. If only I knew where I store these useful reminders inside the old grey matter.

Chapter 11

KEEPING THE BALANCE RIGHT

Another interesting moment I remember well was during a very pleasant and successful cross-country outing with the Sutton Meadows Club, to a place called Keyston. I had flown down, successfully this time, to join a group of flyers on an outing to a lovely pub for dinner. The pub had a grass strip a few hundred yards from the restaurant, where we could land and leave the machines safely whilst we enjoyed a delicious meal. I will stress here that none of us drank any alcohol – pilots are not permitted to drink and fly. Microlights are tricky enough to fly when one has full control of one's faculties!

All was going well until we strapped ourselves back into the machines to return to Sutton Meadows. Two machines had taken off, and the third, another Chaser, was lining up about twenty feet away from me with the pilot warming up his engine. I was concentrating on strapping everything in securely when out of the corner of my eye I saw something stick in the ground just beside my right arm.

As I looked up I saw something I had never witnessed before. The other machine was in the process of shaking itself to pieces. The engine was shedding parts like a tired old tree in an autumn gale. The exhaust system was swinging loose on the end of its safety strap, the air filter was also dancing on the end of the retainer, and the engine was acting like something possessed. Finally, the carburettor flew off and the engine coughed twice, choked and died.

All of this only lasted perhaps a few seconds, but it was one of those moments when time slows down to give the most dramatic effect. The cause of all this destruction was a small crack in the wooden propeller, which had gone unnoticed in the pre-flight check. As the engine was warmed up and the vibrations worked their way into the wood, the crack developed into a bigger one, until a large piece of one blade detached itself and became the missile I noticed hitting the ground beside me. Once the propeller had shed the thirteen-inch chunk it had hurled in my direction, it became totally out of balance, and the engine was shaken demonically until it shed its vital organs and died.

The lucky thing, apart from the fact that I had narrowly missed being stabbed by a piece of berserk propeller, was that this had happened on the ground. A few minutes later the machine would have been airborne. The pilot was shaken in more ways than one, but lived to fly another day. After that incident I always check my propeller and all the other vital components that make up the, not so complex, but still important parts of the simple flying machine very carefully before any flight.

Chapter 12

FLYING COMPETITIONS CAN BE FUN!

One form of microlight flying that I always read about with great interest was competition flying. The British Microlight Aircraft Association (BMAA), the governing body responsible for the control and development of microlight flying in Britain, publishes a bimonthly magazine imaginatively entitled *Microlight Flying*. This excellent publication is only available by joining the Association, which everyone does if they own a machine, because the BMAA also regulates the inspection of machines and the issue of the yearly Permits to Fly.

The magazine covers all aspects of the sport, including competition flying. The British Team have held most of the 'European' and 'World' Championship placings for many years. To help select the team members, each year several 'Nationals' are held at various sites around Britain. I saw in the magazine that there was going to be a National competition at Sutton Meadows. As club members usually get involved in the marshalling and running of the competition, I thought I would drive down to offer my services and watch the events.

As I drove onto the airfield I was stopped and asked if I would be willing to be a 'Navigator' for one of the pilots of a two-seat machine, as he desperately needed someone to fill the back seat. I was assured I would not have to do anything, except sit there, so I jumped at the chance to see a competition from a competitor's seat.

Tony Blackwell was the lone pilot, and he seemed to be as sane as any flyer of microlight aircraft, so I was delighted to fly with him. He explained that all I needed to do was help keep a good lookout, and use his camera to take photographs of certain landmarks during each task. He would do all the planning and navigation.

Microlight competitions usually have several tasks. Some are based on Unlimited Fuel, where there is likely to be a time limit to the task, with the aim that the pilot must fly quickly and accurately along designated routes, relying on skilful navigation to spot ground markers, or local identifiable land marks, photographing them as proof of finding them.

The second type of task involves being given a Limited Amount of fuel, working out the most economical way to get round as much of the given route as possible, then returning at the end of the task with enough fuel to land safely. Again, photographs are used to show how much of the course the pilot managed to complete.

The third and most stressful of the tasks are Spot Landings, where the aircraft is taken to one thousand feet, the engine is switched off (or left ticking over), and the machine then glides down to try and land on a 'box' one hundred feet long by twenty-five feet wide. The pilot must stop in the box or lose all his points for the landing. This is always a good crowd puller, and really does test the ability of the pilot to stay calm and focused. The landing position within the box is the deciding factor as to how many points are awarded.

Between tasks there is usually very little time in which to grab a sandwich, go to the next task briefing, refuel the machine and plan the campaign to win the next event, before being airborne once more. There are normally two main tasks and then two Spot Landings to end the day. Each task takes between one and three hours to complete.

Tony was an excellent pilot. We were able to communicate using a clever electronic intercom system built into our helmets. As we flew the tasks Tony explained some of the techniques involved in looking for markers and getting the camera angles correct for the pictures. He passed on a great deal of useful information about competition and general techniques.

When we landed after a task the film was developed into negatives, which were viewed against master ones to determine whether we had photographed the correct items. Black and white film was used as this was easy to develop 'in the field'. Local amateur photographers are often asked to do this work, and they are usually rewarded with a few flights after the competition.

The competitions are usually run over a weekend, and there is always a big party or get-together organised. All the day's events, mistakes and successes are swapped, with a great time had by all. Sundays usually start late, as there are those who like to fully enjoy the previous night's revelries and need time to clear their bodies of the effects of alcohol, curry, burgers and a variety of other 'good idea at the time' foods. There is something strangely satisfying about waking up at 4.30 am to relieve the overloaded system and admire the start of a new day.

If the organisers are lucky both days are flyable, and one can usually expect the early risers to be having a dawn flight, just for the fun of it. Flying first thing in the morning always gives pilots a rare and beautiful feeling. Usually the air is perfectly still, with a glassy dew on the grass and often a light gossamer blanket of mist floating a few feet off the damp surface. It is always worth getting out of a nice warm sleeping bag. The sounds of the few pilots enjoying this privilege usually encourages the less enthusiastic to venture forth from their sleeping bags, and the smell of bacon and eggs eventually persuades all but the staunch vegetarians to leave their comfortable nests.

On this occasion the second day progressed in a similar way to the first. Provisional results for the previous day's tasks were published, and those in contention mostly had two or possibly three more tasks to try to wrestle the higher places from the leaders. I was delighted with the way Tony performed, with me trying to be as helpful as possible, but more importantly I realised that there was nothing that I could not tackle myself.

I decided that the next season I would try to take part myself, in the single-seat class. I would use the rest of the year to both sharpen my navigational skills, and learn much more about the amount of fuel my machine used at different power settings so that I would be able to calculate the most economical speeds in future competitions.

Chapter 13

STARTING AT THE BOTTOM

I was a very nervous 'new boy' when I arrived, trailing my Chaser, to take part in my first National Microlight Competition, at a place called Swinford in May 1991. But not for long, within a few minutes the British Team Leader, Pat Cole, came over and introduced herself. She explained that as a newcomer to competitions I was not to feel under any pressure to keep up with the 'experts', but that I could always ask them or her for advice. The best piece of advice she gave me was that 'If you feel the conditions are beyond your own ability, then don't fly'. She explained that some of the other competitors were veterans of the competition circuit, and would be able to tackle more difficult conditions than I would feel happy doing. It was a piece of advice I took to heart, and have applied it to my flying ever since.

Pat also explained that the flying conditions at this site were considered difficult. There were tall trees upwind of the small field that created vicious downdrafts called rotor, caused by the wind hitting the trees and then 'rolling over' as it continued on its way. A machine flying into this downdraft would be pushed down into the ground, or thrown about all over the place. I had been warned about such effects, but had never flown from a site with these conditions.

I was not the only newcomer. A couple of other single-seat and two-seat flyers had turned up. We soon became firm friends, as we turned up at each round of the Nationals. Richard Rawes flew one of the single-seat machines and Jeremy and Jan Hucker competed in a two-seat machine.

I remember well the two tasks on that Saturday. The first was an Unlimited Fuel event, in which we had to fly round and photograph as many turn points as we could find in a given amount of time. I did quite well, but pushed myself just too much to get one extra turn point. I returned just out of time, incurring penalty points. I was also having problems with my camera. I had bought a 'point and press' cheap camera, because it had automatic wind on. Unfortunately, in the air, I could not tell if the film was winding on or not, as I could not hear it. The pictures did develop OK, but I was not happy with it. On a later occasion I had a film fail to automatically 'take up' and did a task really well, only to find I had no pictures to prove it. After that I went back to my trusty Pentax K1000, which never failed to produce excellent pictures (even if some were of the wrong 'turn points').

The second task was a Limited Fuel event. I had to fly to as many places as possible, identifying Ground Markers – sheets laid out by marshals somewhere along the tracks we were flying – and return without 'running out of fuel'. I totally 'blew' this task as I tried to fly too fast, burning my fuel inefficiently. I also got hopelessly lost at one stage, heading off in a different direction to everyone else. Ignorance and a belief that I knew more than the rest of the pack was my downfall. I learned many good practices on that first day that helped me to become a much better pilot.

The Sunday was blown out with bad weather but I had decided that competition flying was for me. I had not disgraced myself, but I still had a lot to learn. I had proven to myself that with extra practice I could compete, and I was determined to learn the skills required. It was a great challenge.

I had attended a 'Pre Nationals' meeting earlier in the year, and I was asked why I thought more pilots did not want to try the competitions. My view was that there were two major obstacles, one of which was the engine-off Spot Landings as even experienced pilots got nervous doing these. My suggestion that pilots should be given the option to do 'Engine Idle' landings instead, as they could at least power up if they found it was all going wrong, was adopted. Only those chosen for the British Team would need to be able to do 'Engine Off' landings. This removed some of the stress of this task.

The other thing that I knew worried many possible new competitors was the idea of Limited Fuel tasks, as with such an event it was possible to run out of fuel if you got your calculations wrong. Most club pilots did not need to monitor the fuel flow as closely as competition pilots, and could easily underestimate their consumption. The majority of fuel tanks on microlights do not have fuel gauges or easily assessable accurate sight tubes.

I pointed out that, apart from the legal requirement to have sufficient fuel to arrive safely at one's destination, it was likely that if one got it wrong, an 'unplanned' outlanding may result in a damaged machine or personal injury. Few pilots relish the thought of making an emergency landing and risking damage to their cherished machine or themselves. It was agreed to allow a two-litre safety reserve to these tasks. This made the job of measuring this reserve at the end of the task an extra burden, but removed the stress of running out of fuel.

At International level Limited Fuel tasks do not allow any reserve, but the pilots are much more experienced, and know their engine's fuel burn intimately. They are also much more able to cope with outlandings. They often have special tanks fitted for the events, which enable them to see the amount of remaining fuel, and can plan to be back at the airfield before they run out.

Later, when I became a competition marshal, I realised what a problem fuel measuring was, but I still think it makes it much easier for novice pilots to get into competition flying.

Chapter 14

A SUDDEN CHANGE OF PLAN

My second National was held in a lovely peaceful setting around the outskirts of York, at the old wartime airfield at Rufforth. I have a special feeling for old wartime airfields, there is something spiritual about them. I always become aware of all the young men and women who spent time on these once highly active, but now sleeping, ghost towns. On this occasion we enjoyed two days of beautiful weather – and excellent flying.

One of the lovely side effects of taking part in competitions was that

I was able to fly in areas I would never normally have gone. It takes a lot of careful planning and good weather to tempt most club flyers away from their regular haunts. Maria volunteered to come along to help out, and we had a great time. We met many like-minded people, who have since become great friends. The competitions have a great social side to them, and the clubs running them go out of their way to make everyone feel welcome.

I had never experienced flying around hills before, so the experience was thrilling. I was accustomed to the flatlands of East Anglia, and here I was flying round some of the most beautiful areas in the country. It was magnificent and heavenly beyond words. I was born in Derbyshire and lived in Yorkshire into my early teens. I was therefore thrilled to be able to see the countryside from my little aerial platform. I still made mistakes in the events, but I was learning the ropes, and was happy to be taking part. I received plenty of advice and help from everyone, and felt I was making progress.

It was only a month later that I crashed! (This was the crash described in Chapter One.) It was devastating. I had felt that I was gaining skills in the competitions, and that I would soon be climbing up the points ladder. Now I had taken myself right back to square one.

The flight started out well enough. I was flying about twenty miles to meet up with Colin Lowe and Les Elley. They would have bacon sandwiches and tea waiting for me when I landed at the hotel strip at Hethersett, only a twenty-minute flight away from my base. I was going to stop off and have breakfast with them before we flew over the Wash to a fly-in at a very unusual place. Les was a prison officer, and through him we had been invited to fly to a Prison Open Day (I never knew they had them) about eighty miles away in Lincolnshire.

It was June and the wheat fields were tall and ripening well in the hot summer sun. This time of year and combination of conditions was to plague me for several years. I was airborne early, before the sun had risen high enough to cause much thermal activity.

The crash was caused by my mistake. I changed the landing direction at the last minute when I thought I saw wires blocking my landing. The turn put me downwind, and the increased groundspeed was almost fatal. I wrecked the Chaser, and was unable to fly it again until January 1992.

However, as one door closes another opens. My old friend Rob Alston asked me if I'd like to join forces with him, and take up the Nationals as a two-seat team. It was an inspired idea. We got along famously. Rob, was an excellent, highly skilled microlight pilot, and with my improved navigational skills we became a force with which to be reckoned. Rob had been flying for several years, and had a couple of Round Britain competitions under his belt. This event is the most impressive competition in the country and places are limited and highly sought after. It involves more than one thousand miles of flying over a period of three days, covering an area from Manchester, the north-west, as far north as Scotland, down the east coast of England to the Isle of Wight, in the south, and up through Wales to the west, before returning to Manchester again. It can be considered a real challenge for any pilot, but especially for microlight flyers whose machines are so weather dependent. For the rest of 1991 and 1992 we entered all the Nationals and just got better and better.

Chapter 15

TWO'S COMPANY

Rob was not the most organised pilot. He would arrive in his beat-up old Fiat van, a pile of gear flung in the back, with the Mainair Flash 2 Alpha trike in tow. I would take care of organising the camera, films, maps, etc., whilst Maria would take care of the food and creature comforts, and she would always be there to remind us of things to take with us. We had a big frame tent we would carry in our car, which became our cafe and planning facility at the competitions. Between us we normally arrived with most of the things we needed, but fortunately there was not too much to remember.

When flying a task, Rob would often be so absorbed by the crop conditions below that I would have to remind him of our purpose. I learned a lot about crops and farm machinery from Rob. The great thing was that we both enjoyed the competitions, and tried to win, but did not worry if we made a few mistakes.

On one occasion we were flying out of Weston Park, a difficult competition site set in rolling woodland, when the engine started to misfire. Rob calmly landed back on the strip and we decided to retire

Two men on a mission – determined to succeed (or at least have a good time).

from the competition as the engine needed work. Weston Park was shared with thousands of sheep and was a mine-field to walk round and camp in, but there was also a huge Transport Fair taking place in the grounds over the same weekend, so we spent the rest of the time there enjoying the other attractions. As it turned out, the following day was blown out with typical weather conditions and the competition was unable to continue anyway.

The next round of Nationals was due to be held a month later, about ten miles from Sutton Meadows, at a place called Chatteris. Rob promised to have the engine ready by then. However, on the night before the event Rob phoned to say he had not got round to getting the engine fixed, so could I come over and lend a hand? Maria and I drove to his house, where we worked through the night, stripping down the ignition system and replacing suspect parts with ones from my Chaser engine. These were available because my own machine was still at the repairers.

Rob and I finished working on the engine at about 1.30 am and went to bed, unable to test-run the engine in case we woke up the neighbours. We were all up again at 6.30 am on the Saturday. As we prepared the machine for a test flight, Maria set off as the advance party, with a trailer loaded up with the tent and other essential items for a week-end of camping in the field at Chatteris. Rob and I intended to fly the

Chatteris. Much easier to find from the air.

one-and-a-half hour trip. We decided to test-run the engine on the way. By flying there we could still make it in time to enter the competition.

The engine ran perfectly and we had a faultless, relaxing dawn flight to Chatteris. We were lazing happily on the ground, when I spotted Maria and the trailer in the distance. Now, getting to some of these remote flying sites is often tricky by air, but almost impossible by road. Maria was about a quarter of a mile away, but could not find an access road that would bring her to the field we were using. About half an hour later a very cross and overheated lady arrived with a trailer. She didn't want to talk to any of us for over an hour, and had words to say about 'out of the way microlight fields', plus the crazy people involved in this pastime!

The first task was an Unlimited Fuel one, so Rob filled up the two fuel tanks on the machine to give us over five hours of flying time, more than enough to complete the task even if we ran the engine at full power. He also explained that when he swapped over from one tank to the next, I would need to pump a little rubber priming bulb. As my own machine has only one fuel tank I was not fully aware of the procedure for changing tanks.

The task was going perfectly. Everything came up exactly on time and in the right position. I knew we had perfect pictures and were going to be well up with the leaders after this task. All we had to do was complete the final part of the task, which was to make a 'Touch and Go' (landing and take-off) at Sutton Meadows, at the time we had declared before take-off. We had wisely declared a time with a safety margin, in case any of the turn points proved to be elusive. Rob decided on a very long final approach straight into Sutton Meadows, and all was 'Looking good Houston' until an unexpected silence descended upon us.

It took us both by surprise. In our excitement at doing so well this far, we had forgotten to swap over to the second tank. No problem, we just had to switch over, then pull on the starter rope to get everything going again. We still had plenty of height and were lined up to complete the task. The only problem was that the engine refused to start. Rob shouted for me to pump, and I replied, 'I'm pumping! I'm pumping!' He was frantically pulling on the recoil starter rope, but still the engine refused to fire. Had we made a mistake when we reassembled the ignition system? Had we forgotten to wire lock all the items? Had something fallen off? By now we were descending silently, gliding down with a huge wheat field below us. Rob kept pulling and I kept pumping.

As we descended, I realised that on our present glide slope we were going to glide right to the edge of the field, and make contact with the

A strange place to put a microlight.

raised roadway along its edge. Eventually, I got Rob to realise that we should give up on the pulling and pumping and concentrate on getting down in one piece. He made a masterful landing. With wheat ears flying all around us, we eventually came to a stop.

Wheat ears were packed all around us – we had done a better job than a combine harvester! We had stopped just twenty feet short of the roadway. On the road were several helpers from Sutton who had seen us descending just a field away from their landing site. They helped us to manhandle the wing off the trike, and carry the trike out of the field and onto the road.

A quick inspection showed up the cause of our sudden problem. To swap tanks Rob had expected me to turn the change-over tap to the back tank position. However, I knew nothing about the tap, so it didn't get moved. After a good look over the trike Rob flew off the road to land on the proper landing area, whilst I hitched a ride. The only damage to the machine was that one of the wheel covers had been torn off in the landing. We had blown the task, but provided everyone with a great story to tell their friends. The lack of sleep had probably caused us a lack of concentration that could have been more costly.

Rob and I continued to have great times in the rest of the competitions. A couple of months later we were back at Rufforth. On this occasion we were forced to land out in a field in the hills because of the

Rob inspects a new kind of wheat harvester.

Rob retells the story of the outlanding to amused listeners.

clouds, which had obviously failed to listen to the same weather forecast as us. Instead, the clouds had descended to ground level and sulked.

As often happens when a microlight arrives at a new location, we were taken in by a lovely family and treated to tea and cakes as we waited for the clouds to lift again. An hour or so later it seemed to be improving so we took off, only to find that it was closing in again. In less than five minutes we were back at the front door for more tea and cakes. It is amazing how well total strangers will treat microlight pilots.

I remember another occasion when I was flying the Chaser back from an overnight visit to a barbecue at a microlight site in Lincolnshire, but was forced to land due to sea fog rolling in rapidly, blocking my path back into Norfolk. It swept in so fast that by the time I landed I could see less than fifty yards across the field I was in. I walked to the edge of the field and spotted a farm house. I went up to the door to announce my emergency landing due to the weather conditions, but I could not get an answer. This seemed like a case of 'I've done this before'.

Walking out to the road I saw another two houses further down the road. One had a sign stating that it was the home of a Rodent and Pest Controller, and had two fierce-looking dogs. I decided to try the other house, where I was greeted by a lovely young lady who let me use the phone. Maria said she would drive over with the trailer to pick me and the machine up, if she could find her way in the fog-enveloped countryside. Lincolnshire is a county of long roads and few houses.

Unfortunately, I was in the 'middle of nowhere', so could not give precise directions. All I could tell her was that I was near the local Rodent and Pest Controller's house. I would wait by the road and keep watch for her. It would take a couple of hours for her to drive to the area.

As I walked back to collect some things from the machine I saw someone taking my flying helmet from where I had left it in the cockpit

The fog rolls in.

of the Chaser. I rushed back the way I'd come and saw the lad go into the farmhouse I'd been to a few minutes earlier. What was going on? I knocked again, and this time a very angry young man treated me very coldly until I explained that I had been forced to land due to the fog. The lad then explained that a few weeks before he had had another couple of microlights land in the field, have a picnic and fly away, without any permission. He had taken my helmet to make sure I didn't fly off without contacting him. I pointed out that the weather was the cause of my uninvited arrival and he realised that I was not cast from the same mould as the previous flyers. Once this distinction was made clear he was much friendlier and returned my equipment.

I settled down in the ditch beside the road to keep out of the chilling fog, and to watch and listen for Maria to arrive. After a while the nice young lady came out into the gloom, having taken pity on me, and invited me to wait inside her house until nearer the time. I was very grateful. She was a lingerie designer and worked from home. It was very kind of her to take a stranger into her home, and it was much better than sitting in a damp, cold ditch in the fog!

Maria eventually tracked me down, using the Pest Controller's house as a landmark that the locals could identify and give directions to. After thanking both the young lady and the farmer we loaded up and drove home safely. I have met countless kind and friendly people through microlighting.

On another occasion I was flying to a big microlight exhibition at Popham, situated to the west of London. The flight required a re-fuelling stop along the way, as the flight distance was about two hundred miles. I was flying alongside another good friend of mine, Peter Keel. We both landed at our chosen stopping point only to find a fierce 20 mph wind blowing, and no club members about. We had to sit under our wings for a couple of hours holding them down, to prevent the machines from being blown over.

After about an hour had passed a couple appeared who were walking their dogs. Following a short chat they very kindly offered to go home and make us some sandwiches and coffee. True to their word they turned up a little while later, and helped to hold the wings as we refreshed ourselves. They would take nothing in return. It is wonderful to find such kind people in life.

Chapter 16

A CHASER IS REBORN

It took until January 1992 to get the Chaser flyable again. In those six months I had flown with Rob and Colin regularly but missed my own machine. Just one week after getting it back I decided to go for a personal altitude record. There is a magical figure talked about among microlighters, and that is ten thousand feet (approximately two miles). It is the maximum we are supposed to fly to, because above that height oxygen equipment becomes necessary. The lack of oxygen causes hypoxia, a condition where a person thinks he is perfectly normal, but is in fact losing control, and will eventually become unconscious. The other main problem caused by the lack of oxygen is that the engine is also being suffocated, and slowly loses performance. The Chaser was capable of a well over one thousand feet per minute climb rate at sea level, but this dropped off to a few hundred feet per minute at this heavenly distance above the Earth.

I had not set out with the intention of going so high. I was merely enjoying a beautiful flight on a perfect January morning. The winter is often the best time of the year to fly. The cold air is generally crystal clear, a great contrast to the often dusty and murky summer air, and there is usually very little turbulence with which to contend. I had flown the newly inspected and permitted Chaser up the coast to drop in and pay a post-Christmas visit to Rob and his family. The direct route between Rob's farm and Grove Farm would take me across RAF Coltishall and also Norwich City Airport, so I normally headed out to the coast near Bacton and then tracked down over the Norfolk Broads, keeping well away from these often very active areas.

However, the other perfectly legal alternative flight path was to fly above three thousand feet to get over the Control Zones. As I climbed, the views were so good that I just decided to continue. I often fly at six thousand feet, but on this day I decided to stay in the climb to see if I could make the magic 'Ten K'.

It was a marvellous experience, but also a very cold one. The air temperature drops two degrees centigrade (approximately) for every one thousand feet climbed. As the temperature on that January morning was just above freezing at ground level, it was around minus twenty degrees at ten thousand feet. Add to that the wind chill factor, and boy was I feeling cold!

The last thousand feet seemed to take an age as the poor little 447 cc two-stroke Rotax engine struggled to breathe in this rarefied mixture of gases, that lacked the essential gas it required. The air is so thin that the carburation settings controlling the mixture drift out, causing a richer mixture which can also cause excessive carbon build-up in the engine.

I continued upwards for another four hundred feet to allow for any instrument error on my altimeter, at which point the engine gave an almighty cough. That broke the spell, shot a spoke of anxiety down my spine, and made me think of the engine failure I had had the last time I flew the machine, so I set the microlight up into a gentle glide back to warmer levels.

The descent took about fifteen minutes, and both the engine and I began to breathe more easily again as we reached the thicker and slightly warmer air. I was chilled to the core when I landed, but it was a thrill to have been so high. Once again I felt that I had been up with the angels, and been given a very privileged view of the world.

Chapter 17

SUMMER VERSUS WINTER FLYING

My favourite time of the year for flying is winter. In the summer months the air is often very lively, with strong thermal currents of air rising from the areas heated by the sun. These thermals continue to rise several thousands of feet before their temperature cools sufficiently to allow the bubbles to start falling back down to earth. If they have sufficient energy they will reach a height where the water vapour in the bubbles can condense into clouds. However, they cannot always make it that high and a smooth layer of air called an inversion layer is formed, just above the point where they lose interest in climbing any higher, below any other clouds in the sky.

At lower levels the rising and falling air makes for a flight where constant control inputs are required to keep the machine flying straight and level. In a flexwing microlight this is a very tiring experience, akin to trying to stop a cork rising and falling on an ocean wave, requiring good upper body strength at times as the machine is thrown onto its wing-tips by the powerful upthrusts and downdraughts.

Rather than fight the elements I preferred to fly above the inversion layer, which was a much more comfortable region to fly in. It also had the added advantage of being a much less used area and so was also a safer part of the sky to occupy. I love the smooth 'hands off' form of flying, which is much less tiring and allows for more comfort and enjoyment, especially on a long cross-country outing. There is a price to pay, and that is that it is much colder above the inversion. Stronger winds can also be encountered, but they can be a help or hindrance, depending upon which direction one wants to go. More fuel is used too, both in getting higher, and staying there. However, I believe the advantages of easy flying, combined with the clearer air and reduced chance

Grove Farm under snow. Fortunately the runways are still visible.

of finding anyone else up there far outweigh the disadvantages.

The major downside of the summer, apart from the increased thermal activity caused by the sun heating the ground and the air directly above it, is that all the rising air soon drags up dust, dirt and smoke particles into the sky. After a couple of days of good clear conditions the air is usually so thick with this rubbish that 'in-flight' visibility is so badly affected as to make navigation almost impossible at times. One has to stay low to be able to see the ground more than a mile or so ahead. It is also very difficult to see anyone else flying in the 'dust soup'.

I have often sat on the ground looking at a beautiful sunny blue sky, knowing that if I go for a flight I will be unlikely to see more than a few hundred yards. When the urge to fly overcame common sense I would end up doing a quick circuit to satisfy the craving. Invariably, I would instantly find that the in-flight visibility was just as bad as I had expected, reducing the view to little more than the land surrounding the farm. Nevertheless, one circuit was better than nothing.

In contrast, in the winter the air is usually crisp and clear, and the sun's energy rarely pushes up thermals of any great intensity. It is possible to fly comfortably at two to three thousand feet, and generally one can see forever. The downside to winter flying is that multiple layers of insulation are required to fight off frostbite, even before one takes to the skies. I dislike being cold, the pleasure of flying rapidly diminishes with the chilling effects of the cold. I could hardly bend by the time I had put on all the layers of clothing I wore to keep out the cold.

I would wear 'moonboots' and special gloves that took thermal heat pads. These clever devices were either chemically activated 'use once types', or reusable 'heat in the microwave' types. Both would hold the cold at bay for a short time, but never long enough to allow for extended flights. It was usually the 'frozen finger' syndrome that signalled when to return to ground level for a hot soup and a chance to thaw out my fingers on a hot mug.

Flying off snow was great fun, but one had to be aware of the chances of picking up snow with the wheels. The snow could pack into the wheel covers, where it could refreeze in flight and stick to the tyre. On landing, the wheels would then act like skis as the tyre was now 'one' with its wheel cover. As long as the danger is known and landings are attempted gently there should be no trouble – I never had a problem.

Navigation in summer is often made easier due to the varying colours of the different crops. Poppy fields show up red, oil seed rape as bright yellow, and linseed as a bright blue. Often it was possible to navigate by picking a field in the distance which was on the track I was flying, and then simply flying towards the colour. In the winter, especially if there is a snow covering, everything looks completely different. Every direction can look the same and there is little or no colour, except black, greys and white, and very careful concentration is necessary to avoid becoming lost. Previously well known features can take on a totally different look as they blend into the monotone landscape.

The major problem with winter flying is the length of the days, which prevent outings of any great distance. With the sun setting as early as 4.30 pm, short local flights are the norm. But even with all the drawbacks, I still think of winter as the best time of the year to fly.

I always tried to fly on either Boxing Day or New Year's Day every year once I took up microlighting. These 'special' days draw many pilots into the sky and I have managed to get into the air most years; if only for a few minutes on some occasions. It became a sort of ritual and I always managed to get airborne within a few days of either Christmas Day or New Year's Day. Anyone who thinks flying stops when the winter arrives is missing out on some excellent flying.

Red poppy and blue linseed flowers are highly visible and are very useful for navigation.

Chapter 18

CRAZY MEN AND CRAZY MOMENTS

I can still recall vividly some of the moments when I did things which with hindsight I should never have attempted. They are the incidents when it seemed like a good idea at the time. I believe, however, in the saying that 'If you never make mistakes you never make anything'. I must have learned something because I have certainly made a lot of mistakes!

Off the north coast of Norfolk is a large sand bar known as Blakeney Point. It is normally high and dry at low tide, but becomes almost covered once the tide rolls back in. Seals love to bask on the beautiful warm sand. It is the perfect place to get away from everyone, so a suggestion to 'Go and fly over to look at the seals' had the potential for a great outing. The first time we did this was when Colin, Rob and I were flying our machines out on a trip around the north coast. The sand looked dry and firm, Rob had landed there several times and knew it would be fine. We therefore followed him down, landed safely, wandered about for a few minutes and then took off successfully, without a problem.

A couple of months later, Colin and I were flying along the coast again with another pilot, new to the area, flying his machine alongside ours. We spotted the sand bar and made an impromptu decision to land. Colin went down first, I followed, and the 'New Guy' came in after me. As soon as I saw Colin land I realised we may have a slight problem; instead of the normal ground roll of about a hundred yards, he seemed to stop much sooner.

My machine has much smaller wheels than Colin's and I soon found out why he stopped so quickly. It was very soft sand. I stopped in an even shorter distance as the Chaser's smaller wheels sunk up to their axles. The 'New Guy', also unaware of the problem, followed us in. He made the fundamental mistake of thinking that we knew what we were doing. His machine was an older design with a huge hole in the pod (fibreglass moulding forming the pilot's cockpit) surrounding the front wheel. When he stopped he was literally up to his waist in sand. It had forced its way up past the wheel on landing and was packed all around him.

Now we had a problem, well several actually. The sand was too soft to taxi on and the three machines had broken through the hard shell that formed the surface with the result that they had sunk several inches into the softer subsurface sand. We needed to find at least one hundred yards of firm sand on which to take off. If during the take-off roll we hit the soft sand, we could tip the machines over. The tide was not fully out, and the sand bar was an island. Was the tide coming in or going out? What had initially seemed like a great idea was now looking very serious. We could wade to the shore across the channel of sea water but that risked taking a chance on the depth of the water and the strength of the current. If we left the machines on the sand bar the sea water would wreck them.

The 'New Guy' had brought along twenty litres of fuel in a spare can, both as a reserve to fill up his smaller fuel tank and as extra ballast. He also carried a fifty-six pound weight. Two-seat machines often carry extra ballast to make them more comfortable to fly single-seat. He decided to ditch all this extra weight.

Colin and I walked the length of the sand bar, looking for enough firm sand to fly off. The sand seemed to be drying out, with a good westerly wind helping the process, so we decided to wait for a while. Eventually conditions were 'As good as they were going to get'. It was a 'go for it' situation – win or bust! The wind had freshened considerably which was a bonus as we would not need quite such a long ground roll. Perhaps nature had decided to be kind to us this day. We dragged the machines over to the most promising stretch of sand, after walking over the area several times to compact the sand as much as possible.

Colin went first, leaping into the air rapidly, and I followed using my very best 'short field take-off' technique. This involves holding the machine on the brake, applying maximum revs, pushing the control bar all the way out to try to get wind under the wing to lift the weight off the wheels. It worked – I popped off the sand in just a few yards. The 'New Guy' was last. He saw us go and knew it was either risk bending the machine or leaving it on the sand bar for King Neptune to claim. Fortunately, his lightened machine also jumped into the air when he applied full power. Three very relieved 'Not going to do that again!' pilots headed for home. The 'New Guy' realised that he had joined the Crazy Gang.

Chapter 19

A RAINBOW OF MICROLIGHTS

One of my favourite outings of 1992 was a flight involving a mass visit by thirty microlights to Duxford, a huge internationally famous flying museum with a very active runway. Built on an old World War Two airfield, Duxford is the home of many warriors, a Concorde and many other fascinating pieces of aviation history. It has a multitude of wonderful displays and is the perfect place to spend a day out.

Normally, large very active airfields treat microlights very badly, often banning them as being totally incompatible with other forms of 'real' aviation, or charging the same fees as for a 747. Because microlights generally fly at around 50–60 mph, some airfields have the opinion that they cannot fit in to normal aircraft movements, demonstrating the uneducated views of certain establishments. The strange thing is that they will allow non-microlight versions of the same aircraft to land, and machines like the Piper Cub, which fly at similar speeds to microlights, are accepted. It is just narrow minded individuals I suppose. In many areas miocrolights, gliders, light aircraft and even model aircraft flying can be seen in total harmony, with slightly different patterns flown to allow each form of flying to co-exist. Fortunately, Duxford is one of the more enlightened establishments.

On a lovely sunny morning in May I was up early and on my way to Chatteris. A large group of thirty machines was converging on the friendly microlight airfield for a mass fly-in to this lovely museum. Peter Keel had flown over from Hethersett to fly alongside me on what was to be a wonderful rare experience. We arrived as they were all taking off and fitted into the long line of machines heading south. Both Peter and I were 'on radio' and were able to follow the leader's directions. The squadron was strung out over several miles as the different types of machine maintained safe separation.

Arriving at Duxford, the main body of machines was lining up to land on the grass alongside the main runway, but both Peter and I really wanted to get the 'proper' old wartime runway in our log-books. We called the tower and obtained permission to land on the 'hard' runway, then taxied right up to the crowd line beside the control tower. It was fantastic to see the thirty multicoloured butterflies of the skies parked where the crowds of visitors could get a close look at them. After paying the very reasonable landing fees, we spent a lovely day wandering through the hangars, looking at the exhibits and the restoration work being carried out.

In the afternoon all the machines taxied out to provide a mass take-off spectacle for the crowds of spectators. A rainbow effect was produced as we all lifted into the skies to return home. Peter and I again opted for the hard runway, and had the delightful experience of following 'Sally B', a World War Two Vintage American B17 Flying Fortress into the skies. The whole day had cost far less than the cost of fuelling a light aircraft for an hour's flying. It was an experience never to be forgotten.

Chapter 20

ROUND BRITAIN

Rob had decided to enter the Round Britain Microlight Competition again, and wanted me to accompany him on this marathon event. The four-day event would be the longest and toughest flying event I had ever entered. To get a couple of good flying days in a row in England is quite rare, as the weather in one part of the country is normally completely different from that a few hundred miles away. In previous years Rob had encountered terrible conditions but I hoped that we would get better than normal weather for this fantastic event.

As the competition was staged during my school term I had to get special permission to take part. As I was trying to make the British Team the governors of the school kindly allowed me to take time out. Rob and I packed everything into his old Fiat and drove the two hundred miles to Barton, Lancashire, on the north-west coast of England, where the competition started and ended. This year we struck lucky, the weather was perfect for the whole event – well, almost.

The concept of the competition is very simple: three-and-a-half days are allotted to fly as far round the country as possible, photographing as many of the listed landmarks as one can. The photos are used to work out the distances flown and whoever flies the longest distance wins.

Everyone is expected to find their own refuelling points, but must not have any prearranged fuel dumps. All flying must be between 7.00 am and 7.00 pm. Competitors camp out, or find overnight accommodation where they land. Everyone must spend the second night on the Isle of Wight, in the English Channel. The skills required to be successful in this marathon of microlighting competitions are, to use the wind and weather patterns to travel as far as possible in the allowed time, and to waste as little time as possible making refuelling stops.

We elected to head north into Scotland, then across to the east coast, trying to get as far down the country as we could before the 7.00 pm deadline. However, we made a tactical mistake. As we flew over the Lake District the winds freshened into a strong headwind that slowed us down to a pathetic crawl over the ground. Never mind, we didn't really expect to win, and the countryside was spectacular.

Approaching the mountains of Scotland, the headwind was now rolling over these huge barriers causing terrible rotor. We were being thrown all over the place as we neared Lockerbie; we ventured just a few miles into the valley before we chickened out and headed off south to find fuel. A friendly airfield near the Scottish Borders was indicated on the map as our nearest refuelling point. We were not alone – several other pilots had also decided to try this route. We waited patiently in turn for our fuel, then set off to try and find a different landmark to establish the distance flown so far.

Rob thought we would do better heading east, so we decided to give Scotland a miss. Flying on the English side of the mountains was much easier, and we flew over Wrexham Racecourse on our way over to the east coast. As we journeyed onward we photographed lighthouses and harbours along the coast, before landing on a cliff-top on the Sunderland coastline, just before 7.00 pm. Fortunately the owner was happy to have us camp in his field, especially when he discovered that Rob was a farmer. They spent some time discussing the cost of feed and the price of beef, before we finally headed off down the road to have a much needed meal at a roadside restaurant.

The following morning we were up at 6.00 am, with the tent packed away early, and were onboard and ready to go at exactly 7.00 am. Heading south again we continued on a flight that took us over the

Humber Bridge, through a yellow inversion of sulphur fumes, which led us to the power stations in the north-east Yorkshire area.

Onwards we flew, photographing key landmarks as we headed steadily southwards. Castles, cathedrals and unique features had been chosen by the competition organisers as key distance-measuring features, and it made for a great scenic tour of England on that lovely summer's day. We continued our meandering journey southwards, stopping off at Chatteris, near Ely, for fuel and refreshment. Quickly

An attractive harbour on the east coast.

The Humber Bridge covered in sulphurous air from the power station further upwind.

One of the many stately homes best viewed from the air. This one is Woburn (I think).

on our way again with full tanks and empty bladders, we continued on our journey past the west of London, over Woburn Abbey and Wildlife Safari Park. It was strange to be looking down on lions, giraffe, etc., in England – a very surreal experience!

We arrived at the Isle of Wight about an hour before the deadline, and relaxed watching everyone else try to get in before the cut-off time. After a night out on the town with all the other competitors who had made it this far, which included a huge Chinese meal and a large amount of liquid refreshment for some, several of us went for a moonlight walk along the beach, before heading off to our chosen accommodation. The B&B we stayed in gave us the opportunity to take a much needed shower, and a good night's sleep before continuing with the second part of the competition. After another early morning walk on the beach and a huge breakfast we once again assembled at 7.00 am for our departure for the third day of flying. It was amazing that the weather still held itself together.

We could have headed off westwards into Devon and Cornwall, as

An Iron Age hill fort.

The Giant of Cerne Abbas.

many other competitors chose to do, but decided to go into Wales instead. On the way we passed over more eye-catching landmarks, including the famous 'chalk man', cut into the hillside in Wiltshire and large enough to hold a family picnic on his . . . eye.

One of the two fuel stops we made that day demonstrated the eccentricity of this unique competition. We had been told about a petrol station on our route, which was about one hundred yards from a large public playing field. It was on the edge of a small town and sounded like the perfect place to refuel, before heading off into the mountains and valleys of Wales. Two other pilots must have had the same information, as they followed us down.

Rather than carry all our cameras, helmets, and other flying gear with us to the petrol station, one young man offered to stand guard as we rushed off carrying our empty Jerry cans. As we headed off, a small group of teenage lads jumped off a horse-drawn trailer to look at the strange flying machines, which had just descended into their playing field. As the guy guarding our equipment was explaining all about microlights and the competition we were involved in, one boy wandered over to his machine and stole his camera. The camera is the vital piece of equipment in this competition as it contains all the evidence of places visited, without it one cannot prove the route flown. The boys ran off, with our luckless pilot in hot pursuit.

By the time we returned to the machines a police car had arrived and

Carmarthen Castle, Wales.

statements were being taken. The police car had been cruising by and spotted the strange sight of a man in a funny flying suit chasing after a horse and cart. We all very nobly and quietly got into our machines and left the poor guy making his statement. All he wanted was the camera back, but the police insisted on getting all the details from him, before returning his equipment. The poor guy was there for another couple of hours before the problem was resolved – it ruined his day. We felt very bad about leaving him (for a couple of seconds), but staying would not have helped him, or us. All is fair in love and competition! We pressed onward into Wales.

To relieve the strain of flying for such long periods I would offer to take over as pilot for a while, to give Rob's arms a rest. He would then become navigator. I piloted us into Wales, and we where heading for a microlight airfield called Haverfordwest, almost as far into Wales as it was possible to go. Rob was enjoying the rest and I was enjoying the flying, until I saw what looked like the sea ahead of us. At this point we should have been heading into the mountains, but when I pointed this out to Rob he said not to worry, it was probably an optical illusion. However, a short time later I was certain that I could see waves breaking on a shore! It began to dawn on us what had happened. I had allowed myself to be slowly turned southwards and Rob, who had not been paying full attention to the navigation, had failed to notice my slow turn. We had swung ninety degrees, and now had the south coast of Wales in front of us.

It may seem like carelessness, but we had been flying for almost three days, and it is difficult to maintain maximum concentration all the time. The lapse of concentration had probably lasted only a few minutes, but it was enough to become 'temporarily unsure of our position' as we say when we are lost. This was easy to rectify as the coastline was very distinctive and easy to recognise. The rest of the journey into the mountains proved to be a very gentle affair, without the violence we had experienced in Scotland.

As we neared Haverfordwest the wind freshened and made the conditions for the last ten miles very difficult. The wind's strength and direction could be seen as we passed over a reservoir. Water was being pushed up and over the concrete barrier. We were glad to get on the ground for a few minutes break as we refuelled our microlight and ourselves.

The next leg of the journey took us back through the mountains of North Wales, and for me it was the most exciting part of the trip. The cloud had descended until it was almost touching the tops of the mountains. I was the pilot in command whilst Rob navigated us through the

Wind streaks indicate the direction and strength of the wind, as water is pushed over the dam.

valleys, doing a great job of picking the correct route and keeping us out of trouble. He was very concerned that we would have problems landing if we had an engine failure, but I could see plenty of places to land if necessary. I was enjoying myself!

Flying in a mountainous area can be very dangerous, especially if there is any wind. However, the low clouds seemed to have capped off the valleys to the wind, so the air was smooth, leaving me free to enjoy the beauty of these daunting mountains. I felt like I was flying a jet in Top Gun, as I weaved my way (admittedly much slower than a jet) through the valleys until I remembered that military jets sometimes used these valleys for training. I was very alert for the rest of the flight.

We arrived at our chosen night stopover, Shobdon, about five minutes before the deadline, and watched another machine land just before the time limit. I set up our tent then helped Rob take the wing off the trike and secure it on the ground before we headed off with the other crew for a well earned steak and chips. Both microlights took off together the following morning and parted company as we tried to find another couple of landmarks, before the final flight back into Barton.

The sense of achievement was wonderful and we were elated once we touched down once again at the welcoming airfield. We had done it!

The machine had remained loyal and we had achieved all we had set out to do. We finished tenth out of fifty teams who enjoyed this unique experience. The slate trophy that we earned will always stand proudly on my shelf as a reminder of the fun we had together.

The weather had been the best in the history of the competition, and for me the event was one of the greatest moments of my microlight flying life. The freedom that these machines give is unbelievable. If only more people realised that this sport was available to them, I'm sure we would see many more intrepid aviators taking to the skies.

Chapter 21

GOOD TIMES, SAD TIMES

I was flying a lot again in the Chaser, both in the competitions and cross-country flying. Rob found that his growing children and family farm needed more of his time, so I had returned to the single-seat class. Colin Lowe with Les Elley as navigator and Peter Keel, with my son Michael as his navigator, also entered the competitions. We were 'The Norfolk Flyers' and we had great times flying around Norfolk together and taking part in the national competitions. A great bond develops when people spend so much time together.

On the first Saturday in September 1992 Colin and I flew our machines down to Ipswich Airport for a day out. However when I tried to take off for the journey home, the engine lost all power. I managed to land safely at the airport, and after several attempts to get the engine to run I decided to call out Maria with the trailer once again. She arrived and that night we trailered the machine all the way to the factory in Oxford where the Chaser had been rebuilt after my crash.

The reason for this urgent return to the factory was that Colin, Peter and I had signed up to fly the Trevor Jones Charity flight across the Channel two weeks later, and the last thing I needed was an engine problem. The factory checked out the engine, but could not find anything wrong with it. I collected the machine a few days later and flew it for a couple of hours and the problem seemed to have disappeared.

The three of us trailered our machines to Headcorn, in Kent, for the flight on 19 September, but low cloud and drizzle washed out any hopes of the flight that weekend. It was therefore postponed for a month, until October.

The next weekend in September I was back in the air for the Norfolk Air Rally, the oldest microlight competition in the country. Rob organised it, and Maria and my family helped with the running of the competition. I had helped to run the rally in previous years, but this year I wanted to take part. I wanted to win! It was a great competition, and I actually managed to scrape into first place, mainly due to my knowledge of the local area and conditions. Peter and Michael had started off well, but an engine problem forced them to land at North-repps. Colin was working that weekend and could not take part. Peter spent the next few weeks trying to solve his engine problem.

The three of us, Colin, Peter and myself, returned to Headcorn on 18 October for the Trevor Jones Charity Flight. Michael had wanted to come along with Peter, but he had university interviews and so had to give it a miss.

A few nights earlier, over a couple of pints, we had discussed at length what we would do if we had an engine problem over the water. I was not totally confident about my engine, and said I would not cross if there was any sign of a problem at the coast. We all had differing ideas about what to do if the engine stopped mid-Channel. It was impossible to glide to shore at the height we were allowed to cross.

Sadly, Peter's engine did stop just after he reported crossing the mid-Channel point. He was leading a group of machines across. I was last in that group, and stayed to watch his rescue, but it was not to be. For whatever reason, the rescue services failed to arrive in time to pick him up. A fishing trawler came to his aid, but the machine slipped below the surface soon after it arrived. I lost a very close friend and still look back with great sadness, knowing that I could do nothing to help him. Peter had given his life raising money to help others, and he will always be in my thoughts. I know he died doing what he loved most – flying his microlight.

One week later I had to land, fifteen minutes after take-off, when my engine failed. A plug had burnt out.

Chapter 22

MY YEAR – ALMOST

I was determined that 1993 was going to be my year and that I would do well in the competitions. Winning the Norfolk Air Rally gave me the confidence to go all out for a place in the British Team. I knew I was ready! By now my navigation and tactical skills had improved sufficiently to put me in contention for the top places.

I trained myself by trying to fly to the AA, RAC and public telephone boxes shown on my maps. I had to use all my concentration to fly accurately, following tracks and country lanes, but I honed the skills to become razor sharp until I could find anything shown on my quarter million scale aeronautical map. Most light aircraft pilots use the half million aeronautical map, which is more suited for faster machines. The quarter million is more like a walker's map, and shows much more detail. I also knew my machine and its performance under all conditions of speed and weather conditions.

My engine seemed to have settled down again. Both the factory and I had tried to solve the mystery of the plug failures, but neither of us could reproduce the problem. It had disappeared yet again.

Over the winter I had converted an old caravan to carry the Chaser trike. I had cut the back out and fitted a removable section so that I could push the trike unit inside to transport it to an event. I then gutted the inside and redesigned it, fitting in foldaway seats/bunks, together with cooking and toilet facilities. Now, when we arrived at a destination I simply removed the back section and pushed the trike out, allowing the caravan to be used in the conventional way for the weekend. Instead of grovelling about in the mud, Maria and I could 'camp', eat and plan in much greater comfort, making life much easier. I could get a good night's sleep and feel better equipped to take on the opposition. We often became the focal point for other friends who needed to get out of their tents, and have a bacon sandwich and a cup of tea!

In the first two Nationals I came second each time. The first was at Western Park, whilst the second National was at Eshott, in

Thurlton, Norfolk. An interesting view of the village.

Northumberland, close to the Scottish border. The organiser had planned tasks to take us over the most beautiful areas of north-east England where we were to photograph many of the castles that cover that area of Northumberland. I loved the flying and the hospitality.

The next competition was at the opposite end of the country, near the Isle of Wight. It was on Thorny Island, an RAF base on the south coast right next to the English Channel. I have always been a poor traveller, feeling sick in cars, buses and on most fairground rides. But I have never felt airsick – except when flying over the South Downs during the tasks for this competition. The air just boiled and I went green. I spent an awful ten minutes wondering how to 'throw up' without covering my helmet visor and flying suit. My concentration levels plummeted. Fortunately, however, I improved when I removed the visor, the cold air rush helped me to get back in control. I finished in third place, despite the sickly 'roller coaster' rides.

Sutton Meadows was the place for the fourth round of the Nationals, and I was on home territory. Many pilots get lost in this lowland area, as there are few features to navigate successfully by, but I knew my way around easily. A good result here should ensure a place in the British Team. After the first day I was well placed, and the Team Leader, Pat Cole, fulfilled my dream. A place in the British Team was mine. I had made it! The next day I crashed and 'totalled' the aircraft once again.

Chapter 23

RAPED!

The date was 17 July 1993, the temperatures were high, and so were the crops. The task I was flying was very simple and was in two parts. First, I had to fly a triangle, identifying markers on the ground at each corner, return and land, in as fast a time as possible. Then I had to go out again and repeat the course, identifying the changed markers, then land back at exactly the same time. I completed the first part, and was on the last leg of the second part. I was flying into wind, at five hundred feet, and making great time. I would be 'spot on' and well up in the points, that is, until the engine blew up.

Ahead of me was a huge field, at least a thousand yards in any direction. And it had been cut – perfect. I would just glide down and land. It would be a piece of cake. I would lose points, but nothing to worry about. Microlights glide perfectly well, and as long as the landing area was not too rough there would be no problem.

As I got nearer to the ground I realised that all was not so perfect as it had first appeared. This was cut rape, a crop grown for its oil seeds. It has the beautiful yellow flowers that are so helpful when navigating in the earlier part of the year. To harvest the crop, the farmer cuts the thick woody stalks off at about eight to twelve inches above the ground, then lets the seed pods dry on their stalks in the sun. Once dried, the seeds fall easily out of their pods into the harvester.

I knew that as soon as the wheels touched those sharp stakes, or the cut stalks, the machine would tumble over itself. I tried to stall the machine into the crop as slowly as possible, but sure enough the machine was tipped over, the stakes tore holes in the wing, and aluminium tubes bent and cracked. I had been here before, but this was a very gentle crash. The machine was brutally raped!

The Chaser came to rest on its side, within a few feet of the first contact point. This time I was able to get to the seat-belt easily, as I had had the factory move the buckle to the side after my last crash. I walked away, the only damage a few torn shoulder and neck muscles, but once again, a written off machine.

Hopes of joining the British Team receded as I wondered how to get the wreck out of the field without causing thousands of pounds of damage to the crop. I was insured, but I didn't want to be responsible for a farmer's large claim unless it was unavoidable. The answer was to take the machine out piece by piece, walking down the tractor

Yellow flowering rape. Ideal for navigation, but not a good choice for an emergency landing field.

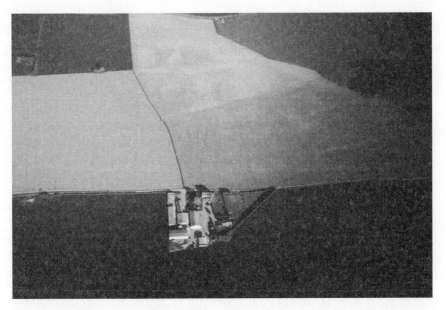

The rape field is easy to spot when in flower, but not so easy once the flowers die off. It then resembles many other crops and becomes a trap for the unwary pilot.

grooves left from the cutting operation. It was not long before Maria and a couple of friends came and found me. She had become worried when I had not returned at my stated time and warned the organisers that I may be in trouble. Other competitors flying overhead had spotted me going down and confirmed that I was 'Down but OK'. The farmer was relieved to see me unharmed, and even more pleased when he saw what little harm had been caused by my untimely arrival into the centre of his field. He did not bother to make a claim for the very limited damage to his crop.

The problem was I no longer had a machine to fly in the competitions. My insurance would cover the cost of repairing mine, but it would not be ready in time. Another team member, Nigel Beale, who is one of the nicest and most helpful members of the British Team, offered me his spare machine, but I could not afford to take the risk of damaging his machine. If I crashed it in competition I would have had to sell my own machine to cover the costs of repairing his. Then an idea occurred to me. It was not perfect, but it would allow me to take part in my first International event.

Chapter 24

FLYING IN THE CZECH REPUBLIC

To get to the Czech Republic involved a long drive trailering the microlight across the Channel, then through France, the Netherlands and Germany. Another Nationals competitor, not chosen for the team this year, had volunteered to accompany me and help with the driving. Jeremy Hucker was a crazy Welshman who normally competed with his brother Jan. Both were excellent pilots, normally seen constantly arguing as to who was the pilot and which tactics were best. They had started competing the same time as I did and we were great friends.

Jan had gone off to Africa to fly tourists around waterfalls in a microlight, so Jeremy was free to come to the Championships with me. As soon as I knew that I was not going to have my machine back in time, I spoke to Jeremy and we came up with a solution. If we were allowed to enter the two-seat class instead we could probably use his machine. I phoned Pat Cole, the British Team leader, who was marvellous as always and altered the entry form. Jeremy was the pilot, and I was his navigator. I drove over to Wales, we loaded up his machine, then off we went.

After a non-stop drive through Europe, we arrived at the lovely town of Hodkovice in the Czech Republic. The competition was taking place at the airfield on the top of a hill, just above the town. The locals were in the process of painting up the town hall and other important buildings, which looked beautiful against the drab background of the other buildings, which probably had not seen paint since the Second World War. The Czech Republic had only recently shaken off Russia's control, and was starting to sparkle with new hopes and enterprise. The people were marvellous, willing to do anything to make our visit perfect.

The opening ceremony was 'Olympic' and impressive, with all the teams being led into the town square by Czech children in national costume. Each held a country banner, and we all followed the band and

The Czech town Hodkovice. The town hall square can be seen at the top right.

assembled in the square. The opening speeches were followed by singing from a choir in national costume, brass band music, a fly-by of three microlights and finally several free-fall parachutists who made the drop into the small area left in the square look easy, as they hit the cross laid out for them on the cobblestones. After a light lunch laid on for all the competitors it was time to get down to the real reason for being there.

Microlight competitions don't normally draw much media attention. Many of the tasks are performed well away from the crowds, that is, except for Spot Landings, which are great entertainment. The pilot switches off his engine at one thousand feet, and tries to glide down and land in a box measuring one hundred yards by twenty-five yards, which is subdivided into small areas only five yards long. The pilot aims for the first area which gains maximum points. Landing outside the box, rolling out of the box, or any touch outside the box scores zero. A landing is when both mainwheels contact, and stay in contact with the ground, bounces do not count. This task really makes pilots sweat! To aim at and land in a box of this size is hard enough, but to land in a box five yards long after a glide from one thousand feet is difficult for even the most experienced pilots.

Jeremy hated Spot Landings with a passion. We spent a lot of time

Parachutists free-fall into the town square.

The choir in their national costume.

doing them during the Practice Days before the competition, but no matter how much practice one does, each landing is unique. The constantly changing winds and temperatures and the tension building up in the pilot all have an effect.

On the afternoon of the opening ceremony the crowds gathered to watch. The weather was perfect for watching, but far from ideal for flying. There was a stiff wind rising up the sides of the hill, which rolled across the landing area. The turbulent air got worse as the afternoon progressed, with pilots struggling to maintain control in the critical last few hundred feet. One machine was violently rolled over, and the pilot only just managed to regain control before hitting the ground hard. I thought he was going to die. Turning a flexwing microlight over can allow the trike to fall into the wing, resulting in a 'gift wrapped' coffin, as the wings break up and the sailcloth becomes a shroud. The task was very sensibly stopped and we restarted it the following day.

Jeremy had practised hard, but when our turn came to do the Spot Landings, we scored zero, landing just outside the front edge of the box. Competitions are won or lost on these points. We were disappointed, but as it was our first International, we knew we were there to learn new skills, and not expected to be medal-winners.

Unfortunately, the next task went badly too. It involved flying along a line until we saw a marker which would give us a heading to fly to join a circle. At the start point of this circle was another marker, giving us the radius for the circle. (We were given the centre of the circle before we set off.) Once we had found the radius marker, we had to draw the rest of the circle on our map and fly around it. On the circle would be more markers, each of which scored points. The catch was that there were false markers at the start of the circle, which were a few hundred yards 'off track'. Following any of these would make the circle inaccurate, and we would not find any other markers.

Map-reading in a flexwing microlight is not easy. The air rushing by tries to whip away any loose objects, so we normally put maps inside a plastic map-board. Trying to draw a circle with a wax pencil on a plastic map board, with the wind buffeting it is almost impossible. Eventually Jeremy managed it, whilst I circled, trying to avoid other machines doing the same thing. It was easier for Jeremy to draw as he had more space, in the front seat, and also because the pilot sits lower in the trike and gains some protection from the slipstream due to the fibreglass pod deflecting the air. Navigators usually have the back seat, which gives them about six inches between their eyes and the pilot's back and helmet. This is not really enough room to read the map, never mind draw on it! Sometimes I would stick photos, or notes to Jeremy's helmet to increase the very limited navigational space on my map board. We flew the circle, but found no markers. It had not been a promising competition so far. It was only when all the pilots landed that we were told we had all been given the wrong centre for the circle. The task was scrubbed.

For the next three tasks we did quite well, but then came the Limited Fuel task. I had been working with a fuel computer on my Chaser to help monitor the fuel burn accurately. In International competitions no reserve fuel is allowed in Limited Fuel tasks. Being able to monitor the fuel used and fuel remaining therefore becomes critical to success.

We had roughly fitted the computer to Jeremy's machine, and it had been giving accurate readings in the other events, so we decided to use it in this task. The objective involved flying a triangular course with an extended last leg. The idea was that having completed the triangle, a competitor tried to go as far out and back along the last leg as possible, returning to the landing site just as his last bit of fuel ran out. All competitors had to land back in the landing box to score any points. The further you travelled on the last leg determined the final number of points scored.

We were performing well, all the calculations for distance and fuel burned were matching. To fly an economy task, a pilot must fly slowly to get the most efficient fuel consumption from his engine. Everything was going to plan, until the computer suddenly went blank; I had unknowingly kicked the power connection terminal off the battery. Now we were back to traditional methods. We both did our mental calculations and decided that we had just enough fuel to reach another marker and get back successfully. We were wrong.

The computer would give a number as fuel was burned, a higher number indicating we were flying inefficiently. If we noticed the number going up, Jeremy would slow the machine down with the control bar. This would take some of the load off the engine and it would burn less fuel – simple. Without the computer we did not notice our slight gradual increase in speed.

Having reached our chosen marker we turned round to head back to the airfield. We were within a quarter of a mile of the airfield when all went quiet. Our surprise and disgust was total. Jeremy landed safely on the side of the hill up to the airfield, and I set off to inform the marshals of our outlanding. We had been warned that if the Air Rescue services were called out we would have to foot the bill.

The old lady working in the field did not seem surprised when a creature in a red and black flying suit walked by and wished her 'Good afternoon'. She was turning hay with a pitchfork, dressed in the

The British Team 1993.

Kevin and Jeremy.

traditional costume of the farmers in that region. I captured a unique 'mental picture' of her as I climbed up the hill to get back to the airfield. Perhaps she was used to having microlighters drop into her fields.

The task cost us a place in the 'Top Ten'. We finished twelfth overall, but the British Team won many of the top places and finished European Team Champions once again.

One funny incident I remember well concerned our eating arrangements. Most of the British Team would get together to drive down into the town for an evening meal. The total cost of the meal, for fifteen of us, including excellent beer, came to about fifteen pounds. The beer was a few pence a pint. The meal was invariably pork, as the locals would not normally eat beef. It was considered to be of dubious quality (even before mad cow disease was heard of).

Eventually, several of us grew tired of eating pork, and craved a juicy steak. We heard that there was a place several miles away that actually served steak, so we all piled into a couple of cars and headed off to find the place. On arriving we asked 'Do you have steak?' The answer, 'Yes. We have big steak,' was music to our ears! We settled down with a few beers to await our much missed meat, but realisation dawned as we ate our first mouthful. It was pork. The man had actually said 'pig steak.' Nevertheless, it was still an excellent meal.

I rate the Czech Republic as my favourite place to visit again. We spent the last Saturday in Prague, a fantastic old city with many beautiful places to visit. However, it is the warm and friendly Czech people whom I will always remember with great affection – Wonderful people in a beautiful country.

Chapter 25

ANOTHER NEW FACE AT THE FARM

I finally got the Chaser back in the air again in November 1993. It was about this time that another pilot arrived at Philip's farm. His name was Tim Harvey, and he had just spent the previous year building a fantastic flying machine called a Streak Shadow. Ordinary Shadows were microlights, but the Streak had shorter wings, and was just too heavy to be classed as one. It was the 'Boy Racer' of Streaks, and had an impressive, almost vertical (it seemed) climb rate of over fifteen hundred feet per minute.

Shadows were designed, using revolutionary new techniques and ideas, by David Cook, who set up a factory about thirty miles away at Leiston, Suffolk. His machines had been used for two England to Australia flights; the first by Eve Jackson and the second by Brian Milton (whose exploits can be followed in his excellent book *The Dalgetty Flyer*). Another intrepid pilot, James Edmunds, flew a Shadow to China, and an Indian millionaire safely travelled from England to India in his own machine. They were excellent flying microlights.

Tim fitted into the farm flying scene perfectly, and we became great friends. We would often fly about together locally, the Shadow and the Chaser (three-axis and flexwing machines) both enjoying the skies. We spent many happy hours flying around the East Anglian skies, enjoying each other's company.

Often I would offer to fly in the back of the Streak. It was classed as a two-seat machine, but was really a one-plus-one racer. I could stand about an hour before cramps would make further flying uncomfortable. Having the brain of a goldfish helps one to quickly forget the discomfort, and I would be ready to fly again the next time Tim pulled his machine out of the long trailer he kept it stored in. The wings could be put on or taken off the Streak in about five minutes, and made it an excellent machine to store, at home if necessary. Tim was dependent

Tim and his Streak Shadow.

on Philip or me to help with this ritual, but one of us was normally about on most flying days.

When it was not flyable we would sit in my old caravan, put the kettle on and chat about flying, or read through flying magazines and flight safety notices. Often Philip would come over, then after long discussions about flying and putting the world to rights, we would wander about the farm helping Philip to repair some equipment, retire to his farmhouse for lunch, or to watch the Formula One racing on television. I have found that people who fly seem to see the world in a very similar way, and over on the farm we all became very close friends.

Tim was soon introduced to the mad antics I occasionally became involved in when a group of machines flew in to visit us one sunny afternoon. After the usual coffees, biscuits and catching up on the latest gossip we all decided to fly up to Northrepps International Airport, near Cromer on the North Norfolk coast. This grass strip airfield was run by Chris Gurney, a paraplegic who had been involved in a serious Tiger Moth crash some years earlier. His love of flying was not reduced in any way by his accident, and he spent much of his time running this very active little airfield. He would have fly-ins all the year round, and always made everyone welcome. Light aircraft and micro-lights would descend on this strip from all over the country. It had virtually no facilities, except for a metal toilet unit and a caravan (which I had installed a few years before). The name was of course a joke, but it was a nice place to fly in as Chris was always so friendly to everyone.

Chris was having one of his fly-ins, and as it made for a good after-noon outing we all got airborne, with Tim following behind me. When we were near to Northrepps we could see that there was a layer of sea mist slowly rolling in towards the airfield. This often forms on the east coast and can roll in very quickly and very unexpectedly. When we called Chris on the radio he confirmed that it was still clear there, so we landed. Hardly had we parked the machines when the first signs of the 'sea fret' began to appear over the surrounding fields. After a speedy hello and goodbye we all jumped back into our machines to get away before it got worse. As sea fog normally rolls in and stays low we knew that if we got away quickly, and headed inland a mile or so, we could get back into the sunny blue sky.

I took off first, with Tim just behind me. By now the fog was rolling over the bottom end of the runway, and I entered it as I climbed out. It was only a few feet thick, but it can be very disorientating to a pilot. Most pilots lose their sense of spatial awareness within ten to twenty seconds of entering cloud, and fog is just cloud at ground level. Entering cloud is the cause of many accidents. I was very careful to keep my microlight climbing steadily and watched the instruments closely until I popped out into the clear sky once more.

Tim did not want to be trapped by the fog and also 'went for it', realising that he was just as mad as the rest of us. The other machines followed us out. Isn't it strange how supposedly rational people, once in a group, always take on the intelligence of the least intelligent member! In this world of rules and regulations it is sometimes nice to push the limits and bend controls. It is what makes us individuals – I consider it to be a part of living.

Chapter 26

TIME TO MOVE ON

Another turning point in my microlighting development occurred during 1994, although I did not realise it at the time. Again, I entered all the Nationals, which took me to places I had never flown before, including Full Sutton in Yorkshire, Swansea in Wales and Davidstowe Moor in Cornwall.

Maria and I would load up the caravan on the Thursday night, and leave as soon as we got home on Friday after work. Then we would drive through the night, Maria doing most of the driving, as I tried to catch some sleep before the competitions.

Most people would converge at the competition site by car, but a few pilots, who did not have to worry about getting back to work on Monday morning, would fly in. This was always risky as it was very unlikely that the weather would last for two days, never mind three. It was always interesting arriving at a new site, usually late at night, and trying to find a place to set up camp. Often we would have to wait until first light to be able to find our way onto the camp-site, and would doze in the car until we could pick a place to unload everything.

Davidstowe Moor, in Cornwall, down in south-west England, was the strangest place we went to. We arrived there at about two o'clock in the morning. That is, I think it was the right place. We drove onto the moor to find a scene resembling that of *The Hound of the Baskervilles*, with mist rolling across the road, and no clear indication as to where to find the microlight site. Out of the mist appeared soldiers, carrying rifles, presumably on manoeuvres. It was a very strange place to be that night! We decided to pull into a lay-by, at the side of the road, and wait until it got lighter. A police car pulled in shortly afterwards, but we pretended to be asleep when they shone their torches into the car, and they left us alone.

The airfield, when we found it, looked like a left-over from a sci-fi film set that had been blown up at the end of filming. All that remained was a few old wartime buildings, on the disused airfield. It was now open to the general public, who turned up to walk dogs across the runways every day. Conditions were primitive, as were many competition sites. Often they were just farmer's fields, with a marquee tent and a couple of 'port-a-loos' brought in for the competition. Usually, the club running the competition would provide food and drink. Competitors took the 'roughing it' as part of the fun, and the locals always went out of their way to make everyone feel welcome.

At Davidstowe they had started to provide a toilet block, with three flush toilets, in one of the old outbuildings, formerly used to shelter sheep. Water for the flushing system was provided by rainwater collected in a roof tank. The toilets were 'cosy' as they had not had time to finish them. Unfortunately, they had not managed to construct cubicles round each toilet, so open-plan was the order of the day. The door did not yet have a catch, so it was not unusual to have a visitor, human or sheep, wander in during the proceedings. It had been unusually dry in the previous few weeks so the water supply only lasted for the first day. However, the toilets did have scenic views, as there were holes in the old walls which had not yet been filled. These helped to create an airflow, which in turn cooled the building and removed most of the sheep-dropping aroma. Our competitions did not have quite the same facilities as Formula One racing.

The tasks themselves were made more interesting by a cloudbase that varied unexpectedly throughout the weekend, even down to the ground level at times. Several of the competitors had to land out when the cloud forced them down. I was lucky and flew around in my own 'little bit of blue sky'. It seemed to move with me as I flew along, and I enjoyed great views of Cornwall. Passing over Dartmoor and the grimy prison brought back more memories of the Sherlock Holmes stories, and the seaside holiday villages I flew over also brought back memories of a holiday there as a child. I did very well at Davidstowe, coming second in my class.

Flying once again in Wales for the next competition, was another great experience. The competition took us through the awesome Black Mountains and scenic valleys of South Wales, but the memory that lingers is that of twenty microlights flying 'line astern' for an evening of fun round the Gower Peninsula, as the sun slowly set. It was what microlighting is all about.

I found flying in hilly areas great fun, and both Full Sutton and Swansea gave me the chance to work on my soaring skills. These are needed to stay up in Limited Fuel soaring tasks, where a competitor tries to make use of the rising air to keep up for as long as possible. At Full Sutton there was a ridge that forced the air upwards as the wind tried to get past. This allowed me to fly back and forth along it for much longer than I would have been able to flying on just the most economical fuel setting. Fearless pilots would switch the engine off, but I always preferred to have power available. It was very different from 'flatland' flying, where the only lift comes from thermal bubbles rising off heated land.

I was still flying my two-stroke 447 Rotax-engined Chaser, but all the other single-seat competitors had moved on to the four-stroke 508 Rotax Chasers, as this engine gave much better fuel economy. I could not afford to upgrade my machine, and found myself slipping back in the points when tackling the fuel-related tasks. This put more pressure on me to push myself in the other tasks, which sometimes ended in 'blown' results.

Although I continued to do well in the National competitions, the new Team Leader, Ian Stokes, thought my machine would not be competitive in the coming World Championships and left me out of the team. Another friend, John Riley, who flew a three-axis machine called a Minimax, was selected for the team, so I went with him as his driver and helper. This year the International competition was being held in Poland.

Arriving in Poland after a very long drive, we stopped near the competition site for something to eat. It seems that everything in the country closed after 8.00 pm, so we felt lucky to find a little road-side cafe still open. Not knowing any Polish made communication difficult, but we thought we should just order the most expensive thing on the limited menu – it was soup and bread. I always like to try the local foods when abroad, but I was not quite ready for the soup when it arrived. It was tripe soup and needed lots of the garlic dressing that came with it to make it palatable. Nevertheless, we were hungry, it was cheap, and it almost filled us up. Not quite full, we were able to read something that looked like pizza, so we thought we would try one of those. It turned out to be a pizza-bread base with tomato ketchup spread across it and then microwaved. We ate it as we were still hungry, but it was not the best meal to come out of Poland.

As a spectator I saw a lot more of the competition from the ground, and learned something about how the competition was being run. The Polish organisation was excellent, especially their marshalling. I was greatly impressed with the soaring task which had up to thirty microlights turning tightly in the same clouds, just wing-tips apart. I was even more impressed with the German team member, who was still up there hours after everyone else landed. He then glided down, threw out a message apologising for keeping the marshals from their tea, then restarted his engine, and went off for another hour before landing. That man knew how to soar!

The competition made me realise that I had either to upgrade my machine to a four-stroke engine, or give up competitions. I decided to give up competing, and build a three-axis microlight instead.

Chapter 27

THERE'S MORE TO MICROLIGHTING THAN COMPETITIONS

I have always liked the look of three-axis machines. Many look exactly like real aeroplanes, and most people cannot tell the difference. I had seen a very attractive machine called a Sluka in the Czech Republic in 1993, and again in Poland in 1994. They looked 'right' and seemed to fly well.

Almost every autumn, since taking up microlighting I made the pilgrimage to the British Microlight Aircraft Association (BMAA) Annual General Meeting and Exhibition. This used to be held around Birmingham, but more recently had moved to Telford. It was a great place to meet up with old friends, look at all the new developments and buy all the bits and pieces needed to keep the machines flying.

Whilst wandering round the exhibition halls in December 1994, I was very surprised to see a Sluka on display. I was even more surprised when Maria steered me over, and said, 'This is the machine you should be flying'. She knew I was in two minds about getting a four-stroke engine for the Chaser, and as the cost of buying a Sluka was not much more than converting the Chaser, she thought it made more sense to save up and get the three-axis machine.

Once I sat in it I knew it was for me – it was so comfortable. It was enclosed, but one could remove the door to get fresh air if one so desired, and it looked just perfect. There were only a few in the country at the time, so I was not able to test fly one, as I had never flown three-axis before. Instead, my decision was based on Paul Dewhurst's excellent write-up in *Microlight Flying*. Paul has been a European and World Champion in both single- and two-seat microlights, yet he is not a person to flaunt it. I placed great value on what he said and wrote, and what he described was exactly what I was looking for.

I have never had much success saving money, any savings I had usually ended up being spent on maintaining the car, replacing broken down washing machines, etc. and on house repairs. I have therefore always tended to buy on hire purchase. Many people would frown on this approach, but it did allow me to do what I wanted to do, rather than dream about it. It meant paying more, but it did let me get what I wanted straight away. I was a good payer, and had no problems getting credit. So, when a 'You Can Have Money For your Dream Now' letter fell through the letter box a few months later, I could resist no longer. I placed an order for my dream machine straight away.

Chapter 28

BUILDING A DREAM

The kit arrived in two huge wooden crates just after Easter 1995. I spent several nights checking all the packages against the check list. (Actually, it was really a 'Czech list', as it was written in that language.) Fortunately, each part had a number that could be looked up on the detailed list. Everything was there, and I mean everything – this was a complete kit in the true sense of the word. The only extra items I needed to purchase were a tin of Evostick to attach the seat cushion Velcro and a set of reamers to make drilled holes exactly round.

One of the major attractions that helped me decide to purchase a Sluka was the quality of the engineering. This was a kit properly

Building the Sluka. The carpet, new sheeting and replacement end wall with window are clearly shown.

designed and constructed in a real aircraft factory. Every joint was properly bushed, and it did not rely on big bolts to hold things together. Over the following days and nights the bundle of tubes and fittings quickly took on the shape of an aeroplane.

I was constructing it in an old Nissen hut on Philip's farm. This old World War Two building, which had housed American pilots, had been moved to the farm after the war, and had been the site for the reconstruction of several old aeroplanes including Philip's own Piper Cub. A few years earlier, during one of the gales that batter southern and eastern England from time to time, a tree had fallen into the building, destroying the centre section. The building had reached the stage where it needed either pulling down, or some urgent rebuilding to save it. Tim, Philip and I had therefore spent the winter straightening out the metal hoops and replacing all the damaged or rotten corrugated sheets. We also rebuilt the wall, which we had managed to pull down in the process of trying to straighten it up by pulling it with a four-wheel drive truck. My call of 'Just a bit more', was too much for the old concrete, which snapped off three feet above the ground. Whenever I used that phrase again everyone expected things to come crashing down around our ears!

At that time I had not even thought of building the Sluka, but the old Nissen hut turned out to be the perfect place. I spotted an old carpet outside a neighbour's house in a rubbish skip. They were delighted to get rid of it, and it fitted perfectly into the Nissen Hut. Lying on a cold hard concrete floor is no fun at all, and when you drop a nut or a washer it tends to roll away and blend in with the other rubbish on the floor. The carpet holds the items where they land and makes grovelling on the floor far more comfortable.

Over the next three months I was able to assemble the Sluka very rapidly. I spent all my free time at the farm, was often there until 11.00 pm or later. Tim often lent a hand when two hands were not enough, and kept me company as the machine quickly took on form and shape. It was an easy 'Meccano' type of kit, and really all I did was follow the diagrams and notes (converted to English by the importer). Apart from a couple of errors on the drawings, construction proved to be very simple.

With help from Maria, my two sons Richard and Michael, and Tim I was soon at the stage where the machine was ready to fly. The only problem was I was not yet trained to fly three-axis aircraft, so Colin Lowe came to the rescue and carried out the necessary flight testing. He pronounced it to be, 'Perfect. A really nice and easy machine to fly!'

Chapter 29

LEARNING NEW SKILLS

I still had the Chaser but decided not to fly it, as I had to get used to the idea of controls that worked in the 'opposite sense' to those on the three-axis Sluka. On all flexwing microlights like the Chaser, the control bar is pushed forward to slow the machine down, pulled back to make it go faster, pushed to the right to turn left, and to the left to turn right. On three-axis machines everything is reversed: push the stick forward to go faster, pull back to go slower, push left to go left and push right to go right. Because flexwings have no rudder, the front pedals are simply used to control the front wheel on the ground. You push the left pedal to go right and push the right pedal to go left, just like the handlebars on a bicycle. However, on the three-axis machines the pedals control both the nosewheel (if there is one) and the rudder, but again the controls are reversed! A push to the left makes the machine turn left, and a push on the right pedal will cause a right turn.

I had never flown a three-axis before and intended to get some tuition before taking to the air in my new machine, but I could not resist the temptation to take the Sluka out for a few taxying trials, just to get used to the feel of the reversed rudder controls. I knew all about the reversed controls, I had read all about it, so why was it that every time I tried to stop I ended up taking a left turn into the bushes along the taxiway?

Eventually, my couple of brain cells finally made the connection! The brake pedal was fitted on the Chaser's left pedal, and normally when I landed I would automatically apply the brake as I was stopping. What I was doing was subconsciously applying the left brake every time I wanted to stop, causing the sudden departure into the bushes.

I spent a lot of time getting used to the controls, as I knew that I needed to be able to operate them automatically when flying. I knew that many pilots who normally flew three-axis machines had run into all sorts of problems trying to fly flexwings. Reversing the controls during a landing was a good way to bury any flying machine, and was not to be recommended. So I would spend hours taxying up and down the runway, gradually getting used to the feel of everything. The Sluka still did not have any wing coverings at this stage, and was merely a metal frame. The practising was also good for the engine to run it in, and it was the only way I could experience the dream of three-axis 'flying' whilst I saved up the money for the conversion course.

I learned about the importance of security wiring all the nuts and fittings on one of the early taxying trials. Vibration is the enemy of all machines. Things can vibrate loose and fall off, which is very embarrassing in flight. I was taxying the Sluka for fun, just after attaching the control wires to the ailerons, elevators and rudder. On the way back down the strip I felt the controls go light on one side, and as I looked back I could see one of the control wires swinging free.

I had not made the final adjustments to the control wires, knowing that I had to remove them later to fit some other components. I had therefore not bothered to put the locking wires around the turn-buckles that tensioned these cables. Bad move! The vibration made the turnbuckles unscrew themselves and the barrel part fell off into the grass.

We had the moment captured on video, but could we find the part? Philip, Tim, Maria, Sammy (Philip's daughter) and I all spent several hours feeling amongst the grass, rabbit droppings and other rubbish in the 'drop site'. We even tried a metal detector, but we never found the turnbuckle barrel. I was extra careful to wire lock everything on

Hangar Flying.

the Sluka properly from that moment onwards. It also taught me the vital importance of locking wire.

My taxying trials went well, and I almost became too confident. Once the fabric coverings were added to the metal frame I decided I would just add enough power to make the nosewheel come off the ground, so that I could get a better feel of the controls. I lined up into the very light wind and gently applied power to roll along the ground as usual, then I added a fraction more. Up came the nosewheel as required, unfortunately up came the other two wheels as well. This was not what I intended, or wanted, as I was now flying about three feet off the ground. I had not received the training yet nor had I not read the next page of the training manual, and I knew any further airborne activities could only end in one, very expensive, way. I quickly pushed the throttle shut and thumped unceremoniously back on the ground. It was time to get some lessons.

Chapter 30

You've Got to be Joking

I saved up enough money to go for the conversion course in October at the microlight school at Sandy, Bedfordshire. I had set aside a couple of days, but really wanted to complete the conversion in one day if possible. The instructors there looked at each other and smiled, 'You really think you can convert in just a few hours?'

The CAA requirement to take three-axis conversion lessons had recently been applied, because several people had had 'bad moments' doing it themselves. There was no set minimum requirement, and it was up to the instructor to decide when a pilot had learned enough to go solo. However, five hours was thought to be the absolute minimum.

I thought I could do it in the minimum of time, but we could only fit in just under three hours on the first day. We flew in a two-seat training machine called an AX3, which though bigger and more sluggish on the ground than my Sluka, handled in a very similar way in the air. My instructor said that if I continued to make the same progress then I should soon be able to go solo. I asked if they could give me the rest of the lessons the next day, and after some discussion they decided that they could fit me in, if I was there at 8.00 am. I asked if I could camp overnight in their school caravan, and was up and ready to go at the crack of dawn.

The next morning, my instructor arrived exactly on time, and I had two hours of very intensive flying, with stalls, engine failures and advanced manoeuvres being thrown at me from all directions. The weather was not ideal, with a thick mist making it difficult to see anything towards the sun. Fortunately, I was used to marginal conditions and did not find them too much of a problem. I was almost as surprised as my instructor when after just five hours and forty minutes total training he said he was letting me go off on my own.

I never thought I would experience again the feeling I had when I was first allowed to go solo in the flexwing, but it came back to me during my ten-minute flight alone in this three-axis machine. I was now qualified to fly my own three-axis machine. I flew the Sluka just four days later; I flew for forty-five minutes and made four landings. The Sluka handled even better than I had hoped. It really was my dream machine.

The major advantage of the Sluka, was its ability to handle stronger

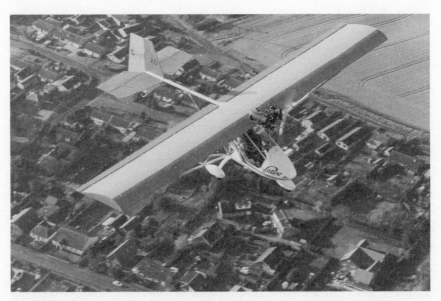

The Sluka really was a dream machine. (Photo courtesy of Mike Page).

winds. No longer did I have to fight the controls to prevent a machine from turning over on the ground. No longer did I have to develop the muscles to fight strong thermals in the air. I now had 'mechanical advantage'.

Three-axis controls allow for fingertip control. I could take on 25 mph winds, on the ground, without any worries about being blown over. The controls easily coped with crosswinds, both during taxying and landing. This opened up a whole new range of conditions that I now could handle safely.

My cruising speed of 60 mph usually allowed me to make some progress against breezy conditions, and I was able to fly in comfort, without the need for all the extra clothing. I could even take a drink and sandwiches with me. I was enclosed in my comfortable little cockpit, with great views of the world – this was luxury. I had found another aspect of flying to stretch me further and I loved every moment.

Chapter 31

BEING A CHIEF MARSHAL CAN BE FUN

During the summer of 1995 I saw that the European Microlight Championships were to be held at Little Rissington, in Gloucestershire, and that they were looking for helpers. I foolishly volunteered, foolish because when David Cole, Chairman of the BMAA, phoned me back asking if I would be willing to be the Chief Marshal, I asked what was involved and he said, 'Oh, it's quite easy. You just help to run the ground part of the competition.'

As I had been involved in the competitions before he thought I would be the perfect person to organise all the other volunteers. Most of these volunteers had little experience of microlighting, never mind competitions, but they were very willing I was assured. It would be great fun, spending two weeks of my holiday on an abandoned RAF airfield, with all the International competitors and my old friends from the British Team. Foolishly I took the bait.

I was accustomed to arriving at competition sites with some pretty basic facilities, and knew that I probably had a week of setting up tents, water supplies, toilets, food and all the other essentials that go with any similar event. The other eighteen marshals arrived over the next couple of days, and I started classes to explain what a microlight was, safety, and the marshalling skills necessary to run a competition.

The eighteen people who had also foolishly given up their holiday to work in this concentration camp for two weeks were wonderful. I organised those who had flown microlights before to become team leaders. Each team would be responsible for just a few areas of the competition, so that they would not have too much to learn. The idea worked well and they soon became excellent marshalling teams.

The disused and abandoned aerodrome still had several buildings which were empty, dirty and without electricity. We spent the first week converting the place into the mini village that would become home for all those arriving for the competition. Cleaning out the old buildings and painting the areas later to be used for briefing, feeding and entertaining the competitors and their followers took most of the week. Water supplies and the electricity were turned back on and telephone lines were reconnected. By the time competitors started to arrive we had most of the systems up and running.

We used any early arriving competitors to train the marshals. We looked at their machines, practised safe methods of approaching them, how to inspect them for illegal equipment and how to check fuel systems. We also practised starting competitors from take-off boxes and judging good landings in the boxes. Most importantly we dealt with accurate timing and identification of the different machines as they flew overhead 'gates'.

These gates are basically two lengths of string stretched between two poles. A marshal would lie down under the strings and call out when a machine flew over the two lined-up strings. A second marshal would then call out a time to be recorded by the third marshal. These gates could be either on the airfield, to be used as start and finish gates, or put out in the countryside to time the pilots past a certain point. The advantage of using gates on the airfield, especially at the end of a task, was that the machines could be timed safely, without them trying to rush back to land. Imagine twenty microlights or more all trying to land on the same spot at the same time and you can picture the potential for disaster. After passing through the overhead gates, possibly side by side (and at different heights if necessary), the pilots had plenty of time to separate and land safely.

However, the workload of the marshals was very high and after the second day of the competition several of the marshals said that they were going home. They had come for a holiday, and to enjoy themselves, but the workload with just eighteen marshals was unbearable.

On the third day half of the computer scoring team walked out, the lady involved had arrived with her boyfriend to take charge of all the electronic scoring. She worked for a computer firm and provided most of the equipment being used. Her parting words, echoing off the bare concrete walls, were heard by everyone within about a hundred yards and roughly translated informed everyone that she was fed up being enclosed in a hot room with computers and being shouted at, especially as she had given up the chance of a nice holiday in the sun. Her boyfriend stayed to work alone and fortunately he persuaded her to leave the equipment behind.

We were getting up at 6.00 am and working solidly until 10.00 pm. Being out on the airfield for hours during a task in the hot sun was very uncomfortable, and we did not have enough people to take any 'time outs'. We were therefore less than enthusiastic when the competition organiser wanted to increase the number of tasks each day. To quell the mini-rebellion I explained the problems to the organiser who eventually backed down. Added to the workload was a stipulation that we were not to talk to the British Team, because other competitors may have seen it as giving the British Team an unfair advantage. This caused even more problems as the British Team thought we were treating them unfairly.

To relieve the tensions after one particularly stressful day, several of the marshals quietly hitched up the competition organiser's caravan, with the organiser fast asleep inside, and quietly towed it right into the middle of the airfield. He awoke in the morning to find he had a very long walk back to the toilet and main building. I believe he got the message, as there was no further talk of additional tasks!

I was getting to bed at about 2.00 am, after preparing both my notes for the marshals and my briefing for the pilots, and getting up at 6.00 am to start another day. By the third day the marshals were so good at their tasks, that I could go out and place the hidden markers, for each task. It is essential that these markers are placed accurately, as a marker in the wrong place could cause a task to be written off.

I press-ganged another ex-competitor, Mary Keefe, who had volunteered to help with office duties, into helping place the markers. Mary had many years of competition flying behind her and was the perfect assistant. We were both very experienced at map reading, and got all our markers exactly where the competition organiser wanted them.

It was only the exceptional 'Let's make the most of this and enjoy ourselves' attitude of the marshals that carried us through the competition. We became a close-knit group and enjoyed each other's company, especially our late evening meal together. The experience was exhausting, but also very satisfying. I have since met many of the marshals again, and looking back, they all said, 'We had a great time, but *never* again!'

A month later I had two weeks off work, suffering from total exhaustion, but it *was* fun! Fortunately, my 'goldfish brain' soon allowed me to forget all the problems and hardships, and I now look back on it as two of the most enjoyable weeks of my life.

Chapter 32

WHEN ENGINES CATCH A COLD AND SNEEZE

Flying around in the Sluka was such fun, I could pop over to the farm and be flying in about ten minutes, after 'pre-flighting' the machine. This procedure involves carefully going round the aeroplane and checking that nothing is about to fall off, or worse still, has already fallen off. Vibrations and taxying tended to shake everything, and one was constantly looking to make sure everything was still as it should be.

I always liked to fly with a full fuel tank, and would normally fill it up again after every flight. This served two purposes. Firstly, I would be ready to go flying again straight after the pre-flight every time and secondly, it helped to prevent condensation forming in the air space in the fuel tank.

One of the checks that I did was to remove the carburettor fuel bowl to look for any water in the fuel. Any globules sitting in the bottom of the bowl came either from the fuel tank, or more likely, from the moisture in the air. This would condense out in the carburettor as the air was sucked into the engine. The change in pressure and temperature, in the carburettor, often meant that ice would be formed inside this vital piece of equipment, which would reduce the size of the hole through which the air was being sucked. The effect would be less mixture being drawn into the engine, or a richening of the mixture, either of which would create a loss of power. Often the ice would clear itself and be sucked into the engine, resulting in a couple of 'coughs'. This coughing also had the effect of causing my heart to miss a couple of beats, and I would instantly be selecting a field to land in, just in case the engine decided to stop altogether.

Ice could form at any temperature above freezing if there was any moisture present, as there is on most days. After landing, any ice still clinging to the carburettor body would melt and drip into the bowl. The only other place the water could come from was the fuel tank, hence the need for a pre-flight check.

Fortunately, these scary moments only happened occasionally, and the engine always seemed to clear itself after a few very long seconds. Microlight pilots are taught to expect the engine to stop at any moment, and to always have a landing site chosen in advance, but it doesn't stop the adrenaline rush every time Nature plays this little game.

On several of these occasions, the machine would be climbing out on full power, having just taken off, when the engine would have one of these coughing fits. I would be at a few hundred feet, and I would coax the engine, with careful throttle adjustments, to try and make it clear itself, as I looked at the fields ahead, planning where I would try to land to cause the least damage. Fortunately, these scary moments would pass, and I would then circle the landing strip for several minutes to convince myself that the engine had nothing more serious wrong with it.

Another time I encountered this problem was as I flew off a small strip on the north coast of Norfolk. I had flown there to visit the Muckleburgh Collection, a military tank museum famous amongst aviators for its landing strip alongside it, and also for the excellent meals available in its restaurant. It is a great place to fly for an afternoon out. It is also possible to have a relaxing day beside the sea, cooled by the constant sea breeze.

The grass and sand strip is quite intimidating, as landings have to be

A perfect day for flying.

made towards the land, regardless of the wind direction, due to the fact that the strip has a large hill at the inland end. It is impossible to fly over the hill and land on the remaining runway which slopes off down towards the sea. Equally, all take-offs have to be down the slope and over the cliff at the end of the runway, i.e. flying out to sea. Fortunately, there is usually an onshore wind, which helps to keep the take-off roll to a minimum.

On this occasion I had backed up as far under the hill as I could to make maximum use of the runway and it was a good job I did, because as I climbed into the air the engine coughed. I had nowhere to go if the engine had decided to stop, except over the cliff and onto the soft sand below. That would have meant a difficult crosswind landing with a roll over being the inevitable result. Fortunately, after a couple more heart-stopping gasps the engine picked up and ran normally again. There is nothing quite like a coughing engine to bring the mind back into sharp focus!

Chapter 33

FATHER'S DAY

The great thing about flying from a farm strip was that one never knew who would fly in to visit. On most flyable weekends, some of the local microlighters, John Dungey, Tony and Mandy Bacon, Clive James or David Ward, or pilots flying home-built aircraft, would land for coffee, biscuits and a chat. Mike Page often flew his Cessna to the strip, and Tim, Nigel, Colin or Roy Bassenger would often arrive to pull their machines out to give them an airing. We all liked to fly into each other's strips to catch up on the latest gossip, which usually focused on the 'hairy moments' we had all had from time to time, with landings featuring highly. It was always nice to see 'new faces', as they brought gossip from afar. One very welcome visitor was a friend from the Midlands, Richard Proctor. He was one of the navigators in the British Team, and had often said he would like to make a long cross-country flight to visit me.

Normally the weather was so unpredictable that planning a long flight, requiring an overnight stopover, was almost dammed from the start. Special occasions seemed to be a magnet for bad weather, so when Richard said he intended to visit me on the weekend of Father's Day, I thought his chances were even more non-existent than for normal weekends. However Nature was in a benevolent mood, and gave him a lovely Saturday to fly the hundred miles to the Grove Farm strip.

After a rest and some food I offered to take him on an aerial guided tour of Suffolk. We flew off together with Richard in his flexwing machine and myself in the Sluka. First we headed east towards Lowestoft and then we followed the coast down to the distinctive golf-ball dome of the nuclear reactor at Sizewell. Turning inland we then called in at another farm strip at Monewden, then into Priory Farm and finally returned to Grove Farm. The weather was perfect for the two hours of wonderful flying and we landed for a coffee break, still in the mood for some more aerial adventure.

Richard knew of a barbecue taking place at Terrington St Clement, up near the Wash in Cambridgeshire, so we decided to pay them a visit. On landing we were treated to the usual great hospitality, with drinks and burgers and sausages freely available. We had intended to camp under the machines that night at Terrington, before flying off the next day, but were delighted to be offered a bed for the night inside Hayden Block's house. This is the sort of hospitality for which microlighters are famous. The good night's sleep and the added bonus of a wonderful breakfast of fried bacon, eggs, sausages, tea and toast set us up well for the rest of the day.

We had decided overnight, having studied the weather forecast, to continue up the east coast to visit another fly-in at a place called North Cotes in Yorkshire. After refuelling (we were too busy enjoying ourselves to refuel the night before), and arranging a fuel dump for my return, we were on our way. As soon as we were airborne it was obvious that Nature had decided to play with us. At about seven hundred feet thick clouds formed that descended almost to ground level as we pointed our lightweight machines towards the north. These obstructions were caused by the unique conditions in the Wash, an area just off the coast, in the North Sea. Undeterred, we altered our heading more towards the west, where the cloud thinned to a murky, but fly-able, haze.

We were able to fly across to Spalding in Lincolnshire, and then tried to turn north again, but the cloud bank kept pushing us inland. It was obvious that the forecast was wrong and the planned route was out of the question, so we diverted even further inland, still heading almost northwards to Sandtoft, in Yorkshire.

Sandtoft is a General Aviation airfield which handles and welcomes all forms of aviation. When we landed at Sandtoft we were very warmly greeted by the wonderful lady Air Traffic Controller, and directed to a parking place. We were able to enjoy a relaxed afternoon lunch and sat happily chatting to local flyers, before setting off again towards the south.

About an hour into the flight, we overflew a hang-gliding site that Richard knew well at Caunton, so we decided to land for tea and some more stimulating conversation. We sat on the grass, idly watching the local hang-gliders return from a cross-country outing, in the now excellent weather.

Time passed rapidly and soon it was time to be on our way once more. We flew on for a few miles together, before Richard turned onto a heading to take him back to his own strip and I flew onwards to Terrington St Clement again, to pick up some more fuel. When I landed back at Hayden's strip the local pilots had all gone flying, so I refuelled and continued south-east to visit the Father's Day Fly-In at Priory Farm. This is a very big annual event, with aircraft converging on this lovely farm strip from all over the country.

Priory Farm is actually about an hour's flying time away from my own strip, and made another excellent stopover place. I arrived at about 6.00 pm, just as most of the other aircraft were heading back home. However, my friend Colin Lowe, who was now also based at the Grove Farm, had also flown in, so I stopped and chatted for a while.

Colin was just taking someone up for a flight, so I decided to fly with him for a few minutes, before heading back to Grove Farm. He followed me into the sky, and was just a few hundred feet off the ground when he had an engine failure. Fortunately, he was just high enough to be able to turn back and land on the strip he had just left.

This weekend was typical of the adventures that came from chance encounters with other flyers. Microlighting is probably one of the most spontaneous activities that anyone can take part in. The versatility and freedom these machines provide is almost unique. Every outing was always a mini adventure, and every weekend we could either live these adventures in the air, or relive them again through each other's eyes, as we sat and watched the rain come down.

Chapter 34

THE POPULAR FLYING ASSOCIATION RALLY

Anyone who has ever built their own aeroplane has one great ambition to fulfil, to fly their pride and joy to the PFA Rally. The PFA or Popular Flying Association is the organisation controlling self-built aircraft in Britain. Held every year, the rally is the largest meeting of its kind in Europe, with thousands of aircraft descending on the highly organised airfield called Cranfield, over a long weekend in July.

Weeks before the event the organisers publish Joining Instructions, i.e. notes which explain how to approach this honey pot of aviation during the weekend. Aircraft flying at speeds ranging from 30–200 mph share the sky as they position themselves to land on one of two, very active, runways. The system is brilliant, with hardly any radio Air Traffic Control one chooses either the grass runway (mainly for micro-lights and non radio aircraft), or the hard runway (mainly for the big boys toys). After joining the circuit pattern one fits behind other traffic, forming two long continuous lines, all landing on their chosen runway.

I had flown into the PFA Rally a couple of years earlier, with my friend Rob in his Mainair Flash Two Alpha flexwing. As always, Rob had been in a rush to get away, after working on his farm for most of the day, and had forgotten the tent. As the very last machine to land that night, we touched down just as the last rays of the setting sun were reflecting off the rapidly approaching thunderstorms.

We met a couple of friends, who had both brought two-person tents, and arranged to share with them. After a good meal and a few pints we all decided to retire for the night, as the rains were now lashing down. I had stopped off to phone home and got to 'my' tent only to find that Rob had moved out of 'his' tent, and had taken up residence in 'mine'. There seemed to be an extra body in there as well. When I went to the other tent I found the problem was that it was not waterproof. Worse still, this inferior tent had an excellent sewn-in ground sheet, so the water was collecting inside the structure and turning it into a four-inch deep paddling pool. The 'other' body occupying the good tent was the unfortunate owner of this tent.

Being good friends we all piled into the one remaining dry tent, and tried to sleep without touching the sides, to prevent bringing in the rain. After vainly trying to sleep in this sardine tin situation for a few hours Rob and I gave up the struggle and left the other two in peace, to find a better place to spend the rest of the night. I decided that an empty exhibition tent fitted out with a wooden table would be just fine for me for the rest of the night. After trying the hard boards for a few minutes, Rob wandered off to find something more comfortable. I found him shortly after 6.00 am being treated to a cup of tea in the Red Cross tent by a friendly nurse, having talked her into letting him sleep on one of the patients' cots for the remainder of the night.

For my first visit to the PFA Rally in the Sluka, I had decided to fly out of Grove Farm early on the Saturday morning, to arrive before the 'rush hours' between 9.00 am and 11.00 am. I had fuelled the machine the night before, planned my route and had watched several weather forecasts. It looked like it was to be a very promising morning, although thunderstorms were possible later. I had calculated that, allowing a thirty-minute reserve, I had enough fuel to get there comfortably, barring a strong headwind. The weather had been bad all week, but looked more promising for the weekend. Planning to leave at 6.30 am, I hoped to be there by 8.00 am, but I was not going to be so lucky.

It was a beautiful morning with tiny white cumulus clouds developing in the early morning warmth. Everything on the machine was functioning perfectly, and my navigation was spot on. Unfortunately, a headwind developed and progressively strengthened, which gradually reduced my ground speed from 60 mph to only 30 mph. I tried flying at different heights to see if the wind was less strong, but it was obvious that the wind was increasing uniformly at all levels. I kept making mental calculations, based on the distance to go and fuel remaining to see if it was possible to make it to Cranfield without refuelling.

I was cautious to allow time for being held in the circuit pattern at Cranfield, as sometimes the runways were closed if anyone made a bad landing and debris had to be cleared. The worst thing I could do would be to run out of fuel in front of such a critical gathering. It was a grave error to run out of fuel and it showed poor preparation and airmanship.

I considered all my options, and decided to divert to one of the three microlight friendly sites shown on the map. I had phoned up a couple of light aircraft landing sites earlier, when planning for unexpected emergencies, and was given permission to land at one, but totally refused permission at the other. This was yet another case of microlights not being compatible with real aircraft. The blinkered individual in question should open his eyes, and perhaps take a trip to the PFA Rally.

The alternate landing site was my old three-axis training school at Sandy, Bedfordshire, less than one hour's flying time from Cranfield. It was in easy reach, and I knew that there was a petrol filling station just a few minutes up the road. I landed at Sandy at 8.35 am and was surprised to be greeted by the owner, Snowy Barton. He remembered me from my training days and kindly sold me fuel from his own stock. I was back in the air within fifteen minutes!

Now I was late, and would arrive in the 'rush hours', although it could not be helped. I would simply have to keep a good look out. As I flew to the marker indicating the runway direction, I spotted three other machines, one a light aircraft and two flexwing machines. Where were the hundreds of other machines I was expecting to see arriving during the predicted chaotic period?

The flexwings fitted in behind me, and the faster aircraft rightly overtook and joined in front of me. I followed it all the way down and landed safely at 9.35 am. Where was all the traffic? People must have been put off by either the warning to avoid the busy times, or by the thunderstorm warnings. It was a delight to be able to land at such a huge gathering of aeronautical enthusiasts in such controlled safety.

My wife Maria arrived shortly afterwards with the camping gear. Part of the fun of this event is staying to enjoy the celebrations on the Saturday night. Tim had flown in on the Friday afternoon in his Streak Shadow, and we all met up for a great weekend. One of the most impressive things I have ever seen was the sight of about two hundred aircraft lining up on the taxiways, departing in a continuous stream that lasted over two hours, on the Saturday evening.

On the Sunday, Tim and I departed together at 9.15 am. This time we were in the continuous stream of aircraft taking off, two at a time. As we both had radio we chose the hard (concrete) runway, and announced ourselves as we rolled forward and climbed to join the already airborne long lines ahead of us, before breaking off and making our own way home.

We planned to stop at a friend's strip to take a break, and give me a chance to top up my fuel tank, in case I again encountered a headwind.

The PFA Rally sees all kinds of flying machine in the skies.

This time, however, the wind decided to help us on our way, and we made such great progress on the way back to Grove Farm that I did not need to stop to refuel.

I decided to attend the PFA Rally again in 1997, and the following account demonstrates how much the weather plays an active role in making every flight unique, which is probably the reason we all keep coming back for more. I had once again planned my route, using the excellent Flight Briefing notes, and had decided to fly into Cranfield on the Friday night to avoid the Saturday morning rush. I had the Sluka all ready to go, and was going to rush home after work, jump straight into the machine, to be on my way by 5.00 pm.

The weather had been poor all week, with thunderstorms moving around the countryside. As I finished teaching for the day, and started to escort my pupils to their bus, the heavens opened, bringing down the biggest flood of water I have ever seen. Water flowed in rivers down all the pavements and roadway outside the school. The water was several inches deep, washing away all the heavy 'no parking' cones positioned to keep cars from causing an obstruction outside the school. The deluge lasted for well over fifteen minutes, causing chaos to the traffic around the school, and stopping most of the traffic moving around Norwich – so much for my speedy departure.

I finally arrived at the farm at 5.30 pm, only to see the cloudburst that had effectively delayed my plans earlier now heading towards the farm. It arrived ten minutes later, continuing fiercely for the next twenty minutes, before settling into a steady downpour, turning the grass outside the hangars into a swamp. I gave up the whole idea of leaving that night and went home, determined to be up and away at first light the following morning. On the bright side, at least I got a dry bed that night! It was Round One to the weather.

I was awake most of the night anticipating the flight to the rally just in the same way as a young child looks forward to Christmas morning. I arrived once more at the Grove Farm at the same time as the sun crept up above the horizon. The air was cool and clear, that is, until I had checked over the Sluka and was ready to go. The temperature had changed subtly and that was enough to cause a low mist to form. As I took off the mist was lifting a few hundred feet above ground, but was still only a thin wispy line, almost like smoke.

I had not travelled more than a couple of miles when I noticed that the mist was now rapidly thickening into a dangerous-looking potential obstruction to my flight. I decided to turn back to the farm and land as I didn't want to take any chance of getting trapped on top of the grey blanket, or to be forced to below the legally required five hundred feet. There were masts that stretched up to over a thousand feet along my route, and I didn't fancy 'hanging myself out to dry' on one of those either.

As I neared the farm I realised that the cloud had crept in behind and below me. I had to land quickly or I would be forced to fly above it, and head inland until I could find a hole to descend through. Fortunately I was using a GPS (Global Positioning System) as a navigational backup. These amazing electronic devices pick up signals from orbiting satellites, and can accurately pinpoint a position to within about fifty feet. I know many pilots who shun these, preferring real navigation techniques using maps, but I am a 'belt and braces' flyer, and on this occasion was going to have my hide saved by this backup system.

The GPS informed me when I was back over the farm. I knew I could ease the Sluka down through this still thin, but opaque, layer of cloud, if I was exactly over the farm, as I knew there were no obstructions higher than a hundred feet. The cloud was now at six hundred feet, and I positioned myself, using the information from the GPS, where I thought the final approach for the runway was. I didn't want to waste any precious minutes flying a circuit, as I could tell the cloud was thickening all the time.

I began my descent gingerly, as I knew all about becoming disorientated in cloud, and was ready to abort the plan if it started to go wrong. Fortunately the cloud, though very dense, was actually only a few feet thick and as I passed through it I was lined up exactly on the approach to the runway. I thanked God, and the designers of the GPS. It was Round Two to the weather, but a few points for the GPS.

I lay down in the caravan, dozing and watching the cloud constantly change its form and texture, thinning and thickening, for the next two-and-a-half hours. The sun eventually gave up after trying to penetrate this frustrating layer of water particles several times, and disappeared for the rest of the morning to sulk.

It was 8.50 am before I thought it was thinning enough to make another attempt. I was listening to the Norwich Airport weather information on the radio, and there seemed to be a slight improvement. Sure enough, when I reached for the skies again, I was able to fly the rest of the journey safely at between six and nine hundred feet, with excellent visibility below the stubborn cloud layer still holding back the sun. It was Round Three to me. One good thing about this particular type of weather was that there was no wind, so I was able to fly directly to Cranfield, without needing to stop to refuel this time. Perhaps Nature decided to give the persistent fool a break.

I arrived at the ground marker which formed the entry point into the circuit, indicating the circuit pattern in use, to find the cloudbase varying greatly every half mile. I had been monitoring the radio to make sure that the runway was still open for use. In poor visibility, the organisers were obliged to close the airfield if the conditions got below a certain minimum. I would have diverted to one of my other possible landing places if necessary, or in a real emergency would have picked a convenient field and landed until the conditions improved.

The conditions held together well enough to allow me to approach the airfield and land safely. Arriving yet again in the 'rush hour', I was fortunate that the weather was much worse in other parts of the country and many would-be travellers had been forced to wait for conditions in their area to improve. It was no busier than the previous time I had been there.

The weekend was another great success with the sun finally coming back to play in the afternoon and evening. The Sunday also started out well, although more thunderstorms were forecast, so I decided on an early departure to be on the safe side, again teaming up with Tim who had flown in early on Friday. The weather graciously declared a drawn match, awarding us a beautiful and relaxing flight home.

Chapter 35

THE LURE OF COMPETITIONS

I still had not got the competition bug out of my system, but I didn't have a suitable trailer to take the Sluka on the road, so I offered my services as a navigator to anyone who wanted to fly in the Nationals but needed a partner. I was delighted to get a call from one of my marshals from the European Championships offering me a place with him. Mike Gardiner was a big powerful builder who flew well and had the strength to control his flexwing machine in any conditions. This proved to be more than a blessing when we entered the first National of the season, held at Popham.

Popham has an interesting layout, with one runway that ends just before a petrol station, and a second parallel runway that slopes off downhill to miss this obstruction. It also has a forested area on one side, which usually has to be over-flown on the approach to the runways. Weather conditions there often tax both microlight and 'real aircraft' pilots, because the rotor rolling over these woods creates very confused air in the landing area.

In all my years of flying I have never encountered such violent conditions as we encountered during the tasks on the first day. I really thought we were going to crash several times during the landing approach, and it was only Mike's incredible strength and skill that prevented us from being flung into the ground. He very sensibly decided to withdraw from the rest of the competition. Shortly afterwards the competition was cancelled.

The next National was cancelled due to bad weather, so we met up again for the third planned competition held at Swansea, The flying was, as always in this country, awesome as we headed off into the Black Mountains to find markers and navigate ourselves to a chosen landing site tucked in-between two hills. Once again Mike flew expertly, and I

The Welsh Mountains are not the best place to make an emergency landing.

navigated us through this beautiful countryside. The problem was that I didn't feel happy, as we flew along I realised that I was missing the thrill of flying competitions myself. I should be doing this in my own machine, or not at all.

After leaving the stopover site in the hills we set off on the second part of the task, which would eventually take us back to Swansea. Then the engine started to misfire and lose power. We were right over the mountainous region, where landing sites were few and far between. There were hardly any places that could have been considered ideal as emergency landing places, but we hopped from one potential survivable landing place to the next for almost an hour. We tried to keep the engine running on willpower – and prayers.

After a nerve-racking sixty minutes we made it back to the runway at Swansea, and gathered the engine experts to diagnose the problem. The consensus of opinion was that the crankshaft was failing, and could have snapped at any moment. We could have had a catastrophic engine failure, and we both felt like the angels had been helping us. Once again we had to withdraw from the rest of the competition.

The competition was a turning point. I had decided during the flight back, that as I could not compete in my own machine, it was time to move away from competitions. I had enjoyed them, made many new friends, and over the years I had flown in beautiful parts of Britain, but now I realised that it was time to concentrate on other areas of this wonderful sport. I wanted to do more cross-country flying, and would spend my time and energy preparing the Sluka to be able to do just that.

Chapter 36

TURKEY – A LAND OF UNEXPECTED OPPORTUNITY

Although I was no longer involved with competitions as a competitor, the competitions had not released me completely. In May 1996 I received a call from David Cole, the BMAA president, and one of the organisers of a new venture called the World Air Games. The Games were proposed as a series of Olympic-style competitions, not only for microlights, but for all other airsports, from all over the world. The idea was that every four years a country would host World-class games for every type of airsport, including activities such as gliding, aerobatics, free-fall parachuting, radio-controlled models, hang-gliding, microlighting and powered paragliding, to name just a few. These activities would take place, during the same week, in different parts of the same country. A Practice Week before the competition would allow competitors to get used to the area they would be using. Turkey had offered itself to host the very first event.

David had phoned me to ask if I would be interested in going out to Turkey as Chief Marshal, to train Turkish students in a practice event for these first ever World Air Games, scheduled for 1997. The Turkish Aeronautical Organisation had never held any microlight competitions before and wanted someone with experience to train its marshals.

I would need to take two weeks off work as the 'First Air Games Microlight Championship Test Event/Open Turkish National Microlight Championship 1996 Games', as the event was officially called, would take place a week after all the schools in England reopened for the autumn term. It was too good an experience to miss! I applied for leave, and dug out my old notes from the Little Rissington Championship to remind myself of some of the problems, and possible solutions, that I may be facing once again.

I would be getting about twenty Turkish aeronautical study students, who could understand, if not speak, English, which is the accepted language for aviation worldwide. They had no previous understanding of microlight flying, but were very intelligent youngsters and willing to get fully involved.

It turned out that there was a clash of dates between the Practice World Air Games and the existing World Microlight Championships, being held in South Africa. The World Championships had taken place a few weeks before the date chosen for the Turkish Games, therefore many of the normal competitors still had their machines 'in transit' and so were unable to attend this practice competition. However, twelve machines, from three European countries managed to get to the Practice World Air Games, which was enough to train the marshals and run a successful practice competition.

This competition was completely different from the ones I was used to. Normally at National and European competitions, everyone brings tents or caravans to sleep in, and facilities are minimal. In Turkey we were given a nice commercial airfield, with a two thousand-foot concrete runway, situated just below the ruins of Ephesus. We were transported every day from a pleasant hotel on the coast, complete with beach, swimming pool and excellent food.

Although we only had twelve machines, I was able to explain all about them, how they worked, the dangers involved in being near them and the way to examine and marshal them during the tasks. The students were wonderful, intelligent and very quick to learn. I was able

Some of the Turkish marshals and I pose for photographs.

to train teams to handle all the tasks the competition organiser could throw up at us.

The young students were outstanding, and made my job a real holiday. Most of them spoke and understood English well, and they were committed to doing a perfect job. By the middle of the week they would all go out to get on with their allotted tasks, without any input from me other than the normal Marshals' Briefings held just after the Pilots' Briefings each day. Everything ran like clockwork.

On the final Friday one of the other competition officials came out and took me off the runway, leaving the marshals on their own. I was put on a coach and taken on a personally guided tour of the ruins of Ephesus. On the Sunday after the competition all the organisers, competitors and marshals were taken on a day out to visit all the famous tourist sites in the area. The Turkish people certainly knew how to entertain us.

I was invited, once again as Chief Marshal, for the actual first World Air Games in September 1997. I took special leave of absence and flew out as before, with another marshal and good friend, on Turkish Airlines. We were met at the local airport and taken straight to our hotel. Once again we were accommodated in a very pleasant tourist hotel. The parachuting competition was taking place at Ephesus, so we were taken further into the country to a town called Adyn.

An informal group photo of the wonderful marshals.

122

With many more countries taking part in this prestigious event this was going to be a big competition. The competitors brought with them eighty microlights and about twenty powered paragliders. To cope with my tasks I had specially asked for two Assistant Chief Marshals, Mike Collins and Patrick Byrne. Mike had been an excellent marshal at the Little Rissington competition in 1993 and Patrick, an enormously friendly and popular Irishman, had helped me in Turkey the previous year. Both were needed to spread the workload, and were given special areas to control. Patrick was 'our man in the field'; he would get up before dawn and lead a team of marshals into the countryside to put down markers and set up timing gates. Mike was in charge of the actual 'timing teams' of marshals, and also helped me control the activities on the airfield. All three of us were constantly busy, but it was far less stressful than the Little Rissington competition.

I had asked for thirty marshals, to avoid the overload problem, but due to a misunderstanding only got fifteen, with an extra four after the competition started. Fortunately about eight of them were the students who helped the previous year, and I was able to put them in charge of the various teams.

We spent the first week learning all about the safety, inspection and control techniques they would need to marshal the competition. In the mornings we held classes to train the marshals and in the afternoon we carried out preparation work such as marking out take-off/landing boxes on the concrete runway, setting up timing gates and practising the marshalling activities. With so few marshals we were seriously understaffed, but the students once again did everything they could to make the competition run smoothly. Patrick, Mike and I were kept busy from dawn until well after sunset almost every evening, but with three of us we were able to carry out our roles very effectively.

Coming off the runway from the day's task, and then attending the Pilots' Briefing meant that we normally had not eaten, possibly since breakfast. Because we normally had not had a chance to grab any food, I would encourage the competitors to bring sandwiches, cakes and drink to the sessions which normally lasted about three-and-a-half hours. Quite a party atmosphere would develop in the petrol-fumed hangar. Patrick and his team would still be out in the countryside, either collecting or putting out markers. He was very good at persuading members of the local villages to provide him and his team with food and refreshment.

When a Limited Fuel event was being run the following day, Mike and I would be found in a hangar the previous night, weighing fuel and sealing containers. This was in preparation for the following early morning session filling and sealing of aircraft fuel tanks.

Limited Fuel competitions are a real chore for marshals. All competitors should completely empty their fuel tanks and present them for inspection, before the marshals allow the previously weighed fuel to be put into the aircraft tanks. Then the marshals have all openings carefully sealed and wire locked, to prevent any additional fuel being added later. Unfortunately, there were always some competitors who tried to gain an advantage by leaving some fuel in the tanks, hoping it would not be noticed.

This is where I pulled out my secret weapon! It was a simple siphon device, which could accurately measure any fuel left in the tanks. To dissuade these competitors I had successfully asked for a new rule to be added to the competition, which stated we could deduct five hundred points from any competitor who had more than a few milli-litres left in a tank. Some fuel in the tank was inevitable as fuel would run back out of fuel lines. This tiny amount of fuel was permissible, but more than that brought down the wrath of the Chief Marshal on the pilot concerned. It was wonderful to see a whole group of competitors rapidly pull out of the waiting line to recheck their tanks, after we penalised the first competitor who tried to fool us. He had almost a litre of fuel in his tank. We never had any more problems with extra fuel when inspecting tanks.

The inspection, fuelling and sealing of tanks was very time-consuming. Starting at 7.00 am we struggled to finish all eighty machines by 12.00 pm. Mike, Patrick and all the marshals would do the main body of this work, and I would also inspect and seal some of them. I would then finally recheck seals and sign them off, before allowing a machine to be taken to the start line.

The most spectacular sight from this competition, and one I will always cherish, was when we had to try to get all eighty machines into the air safely for a Limited Fuel Soaring task. All the pilots had waited until the conditions were perfect and then simultaneously pulled out four abreast, to be marshalled into the single take-off box, to be on their way. It was an awesome sight. My only regret is that I ran out of film just before the event started and could not capture the moment for posterity.

The first World Air Games were a huge success, largely due to the excellent young Turkish marshals, and all the other people who worked so hard to sort out any problems. It was a privilege to work with such wonderful, cheerful and dedicated young men and women.

Chapter 37

FLYING FOR THE FUN OF IT

When flying one doesn't always have to be going somewhere. Many of us take to the skies for a flight lasting possibly thirty minutes or so, just for the fun of it. Sometimes the conditions on the ground seem ideal, but as soon as the machine is airborne, it becomes obvious that the conditions above ground are totally different. A pilot may therefore try out different heights, hoping to find smoother air, or decide to give up and try later. Often though it is the need to get back into the air that is the fix we crave. Once airborne we feel 'at one' and relax as the earth-bound worries and concerns fall away.

Another favourite moment I remember vividly is when I decided to go flying on 1 January 1998. On the ground there was a fitful wind

A group of friends fly in to visit at Grove Farm.

gusting between 15–20 mph, but it was New Year's Day, and I always like to fly at the end and start of every year. I decided to go and play anyway.

I knew the wind would be stronger as I climbed higher, but I was determined to get my fix. At about one thousand feet I found that I could slow right down and hover. The wind-speed was equal to my airspeed, so it looked like I was suspended in the air. I looked down and picked out an object on the ground, to see if I really was stationary – I was. I gently eased the controls over to one side and floated sideways. This was fun!

Next I tried reducing the power, slowing down a little more, and found I could fly backwards. I spent the next twenty minutes simply drawing box shapes as I slid sideways and back and forth in the sky, above Grove Farm. Philip and Tim watched from below as I performed these pointless, but fun, manoeuvres.

Microlight flying may not get a person from one place to another in a hurry, or have the same levels of comfort as a light aircraft, or a commercial airliner, nor is it a pastime for wet and windy days. But when the conditions are right it is *fun*, and the sky is a wonderful playground.

Chapter 38

WHAT ARE YOU WAITING FOR?

The thrill of flying is something that many people never realise is open to them. Modern materials and construction techniques have led to the development of many new cheaper forms of aviation. Hang-gliding and paragliding are available to those who prefer engine-less flight. A paraglider is small and light enough to be carried in a backpack up any convenient hill, before being used to take the pilot soaring for as long as conditions and pilot skill permit. The sport seems to be taking over from the more rigid older, but no less exciting, sport of hang-gliding. Many pilots do both of these 'fly like a bird' pastimes. If you want to experience relatively cheap flying go to one of the many training centres and try a one-day or weekend course. However, beware as you may be doing something that will change your life!

The development of cheap, lightweight and increasingly reliable engines has allowed the sport of single- and two-seat microlighting to thrive. More and more people are trying out this cheaper alternative to 'real' aeroplanes. I know several commercial pilots who fly microlights just for fun.

A more recent addition to the growing methods of becoming airborne is the Powered Paraglider (PPG), which allows people who do not live near hills to take up this exciting sport. An engine unit is strapped onto a person's back, and within a few steps a person can be flying, looking for thermals. If they find one they can, if they wish, switch off the engine and soar. Once the thermal collapses the engine is restarted to take the pilot where ever he, or she, would like to go. Take-off and landing areas are small, and only need to be clear of any obstructions. Pilots are able to carry these machines around in the back of a car, or even as hand luggage on many airlines when travelling

See you up there!

on vacation. They must be the most portable of all flying machines.

I recently moved to the United States to live, and I am now looking to find a way of getting back into the sky. The regulations are very different in the US. An ultralight, as they are called, is classified as a one-place machine weighing less than 254 lb and capable of speeds of less then 63 mph. It can only carry five US gallons of fuel. However, it can be flown without any licence. Two-seat machines are not allowed.

I sold my Sluka when I moved over here, and I am thinking of building one of the many excellent ultralights available in the US from a set of plans. It may take a long time to build, but I still dream of flying with the angels again. Hopefully, before long the dream will once more become a reality.

Glossary

AX-3 3-axis stick and rudder two-seat machine. Often used for training. Made by Pegasus Aviation.

BMAA British Microlight Aircraft Association. The controlling body for microlighting in the UK. If you want to try microlighting contact them. Address: The Bullring, Deddington, Banbury, Oxford OX15 0TT.

Chaser Single-seat high performance flexwing machine. Made by Pegasus Aviation. They also make two-seat machines.

Control bar Used in a flexwing machine to slow/speed up flight and make turns by moving the trike unit around.

Flash 2 Alpha One of several two-seat flexwing machines made by Mainair Sports Ltd.

Flexwing/Weightshift Derived from a hang-glider. Uses a control bar to change direction. Foot pedals for steering on the ground only. Moving the trike unit under the wing causes changes in speed/direction.

Four-stroke engine Only needs petrol. Has its own lubrication system.

Licence Microlighting in England requires a licence. Currently 25 hours of training. Contact BMAA for details.

Microlight The current definition is a machine with a total weight not exceeding 390 kg, a wing loading not exceeding 25 kg/sq.m, a maximum fuel capacity of 50 litres, and able to carry one or two people. A new definition is being considered to raise the weight limits to 390 kg (single-seat) and 450 kg (two-seat).

Microlight Flying **magazine** Published by the BMAA. Not available from newsagents. Contact BMAA.

Minimax Single-seat 3-axis machine. Built from wooden kit or plans.

PFA Popular Flying Association. Controlling body for most homebuilt aircraft in the UK. Address: Terminal Building, Shoreham Airport, Shoreham-by-Sea, W. Sussex, BN43 5FF.

Sluka Single-seat 3-axis machine. Mainly metal and Dacron. Imported as a kit.

Trike The wheeled unit under the wing containing pilot, navigator, engine, etc.

Two-stroke engine Uses a mixture of petrol and oil.

Ultralight (USA) A one-place machine weighing less than 254 lb, flying at 63 mph max., a stall below 28 mph, and carrying no more than 5 gallons of fuel.

3-axis Looks like a 'standard' aeroplane. Uses conventional ailerons, elevators and rudder to change direction. Has foot rudder pedals and a stick.

Index